Welcome to my world of Weirdies

*This is the first weirdies book of year 2 of Color A Weirdie A Day,
join us for daily coloring with either me or one of the wonderful guesthosts
at the group www.facebook.com/groups/ColorAWeirdieADay,
and check out all the beautiful colored !
The set has 12 books Weirdies 13 to Weirdies 24, one book for each month
with a Weirdie for each day, additionally all Weirdies are repeated in the
back of the book in their upside_down versions ...
Your Weirdie can drastically change and turn in to a brand new Weirdie.
Get your Weirdie on and have a fun and relaxing time with coloring it,
join the group and show your colored, join the live coloring and have fun
with us ... if you like !*

Weirdies 1 to 12 were colored live in 2018 January 1st to December 31st

*Weirdies 13 will be colored in January 2019 Daily
Weirdies 14 will be colored in Febuary 2019 Daily
Weirdies 15 will be colored in March 2019 Daily
Weirdies 16 will be colored in April 2019 Daily
Weirdies 17 will be colored in May 2019 Daily
Weirdies 18 will be colored in June 2019 Daily
Weirdies 19 will be colored in July 2019 Daily
Weirdies 20 will be colored in August 2019 Daily
Weirdies 21 will be colored in September 2019 Daily
Weirdies 22 will be colored in October 2019 Daily*

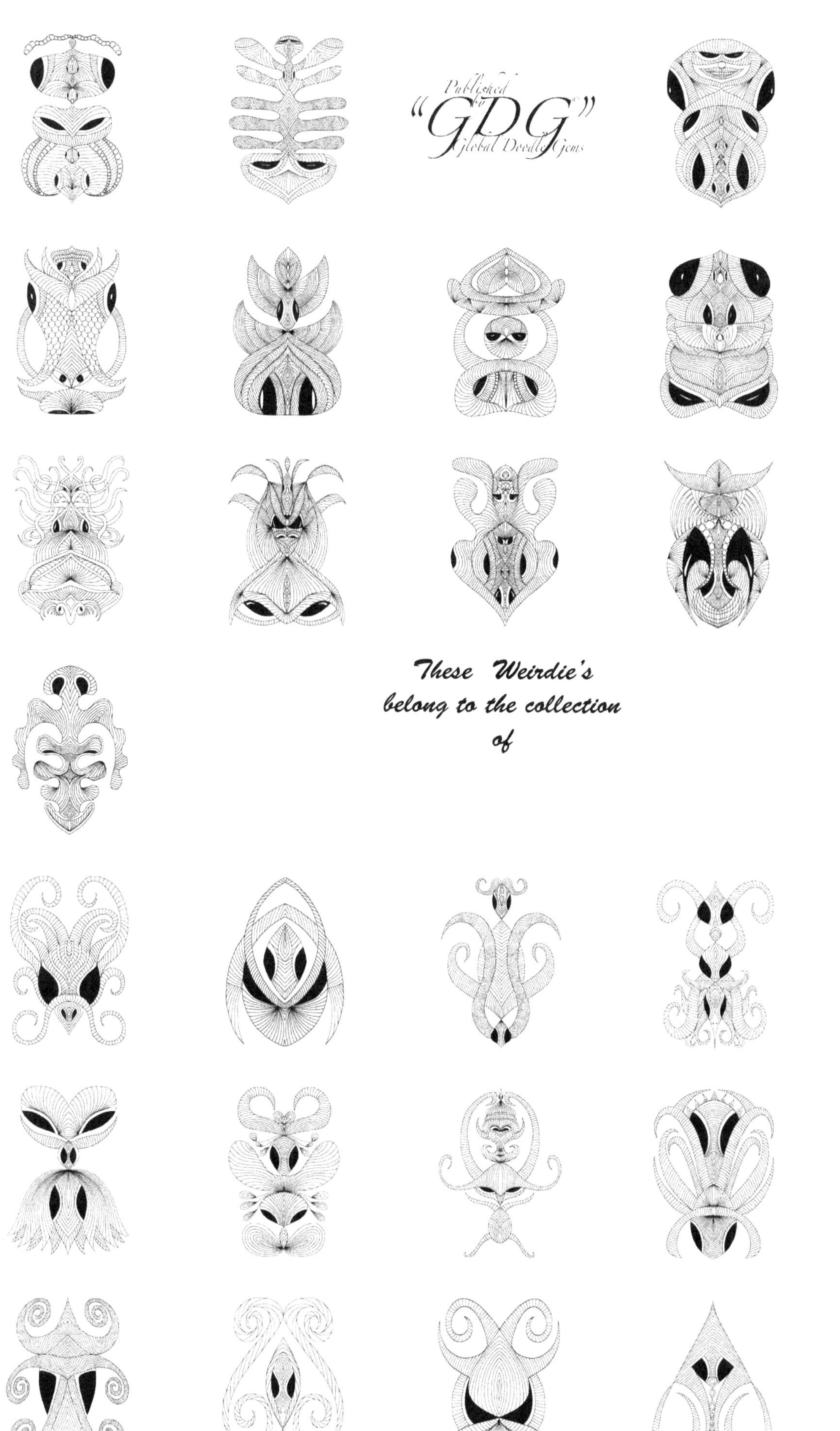
Published
by
"GDG"
Global Doodle Gems

These Weirdie's
belong to the collection
of

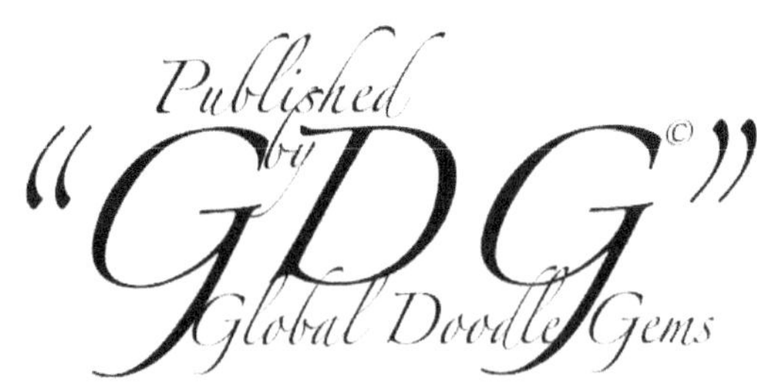

Share your colored versions with us ! We love seeing your results

and hearing from you

we are social !

The Official FB book page, stay on top of what we have in the works !
www.facebook.com/globaldoodlegems
The Community group, share your colored pages, meet the artists, enjoy exclusive freebies, take
part in community Charity books and so much more......
www.facebook.com/groups/globaldoodlegems/
Follow us on Twitter.... @GlobalDoodlegem
We are on Instagram too
@globaldoodlegems for instagram
...and if you are not social like that we have a blog
globaldoodlegems.wordpress.com

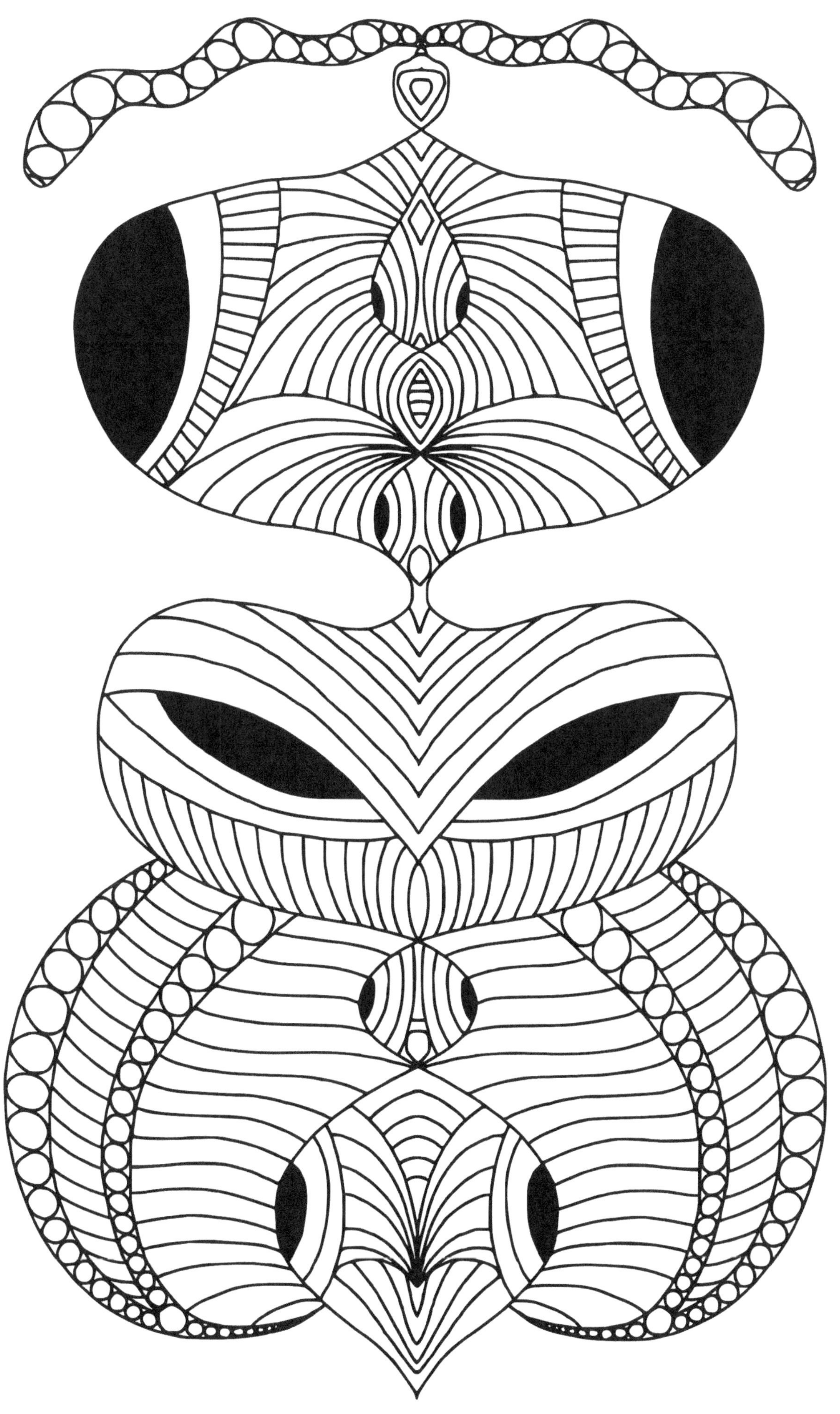

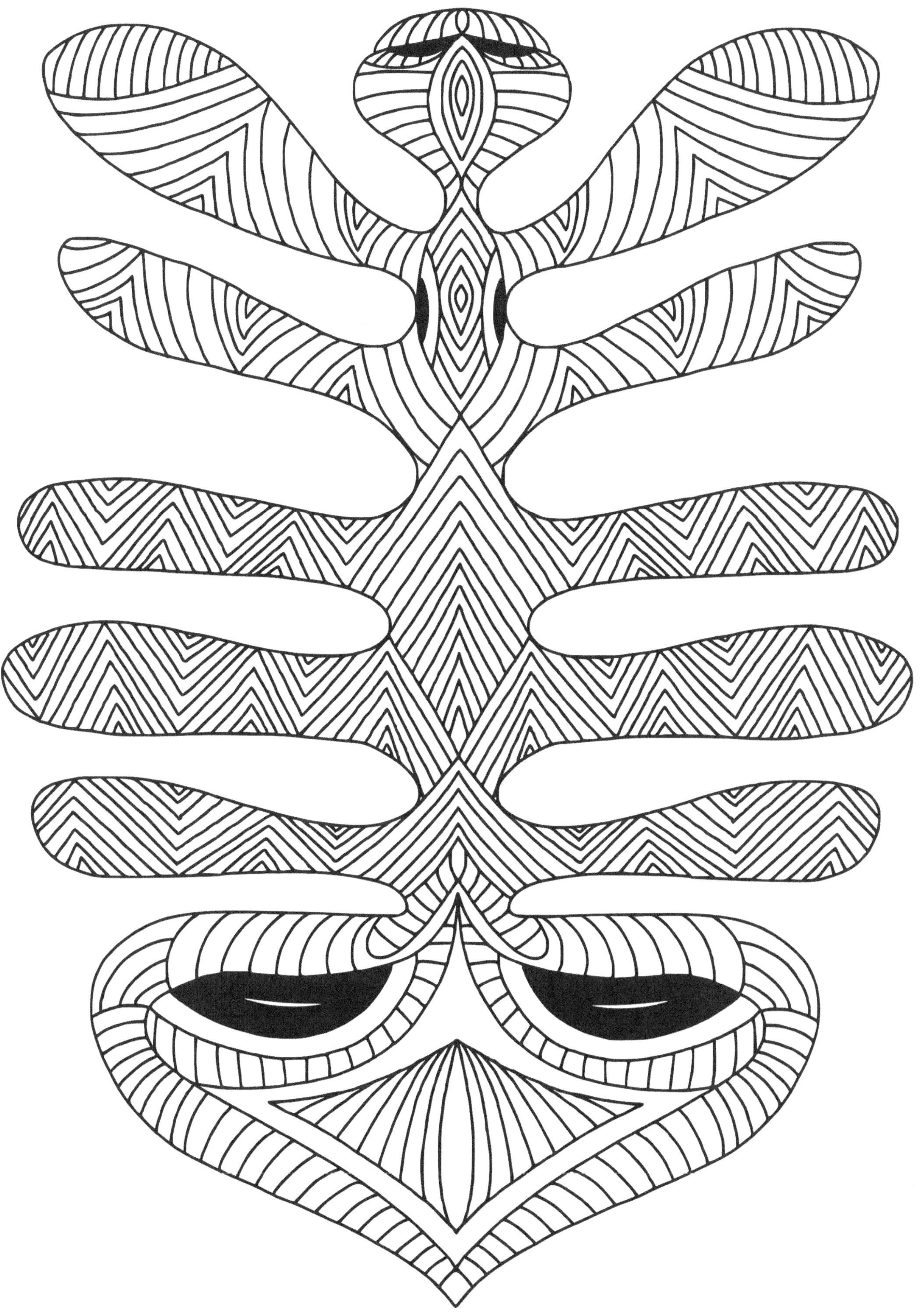

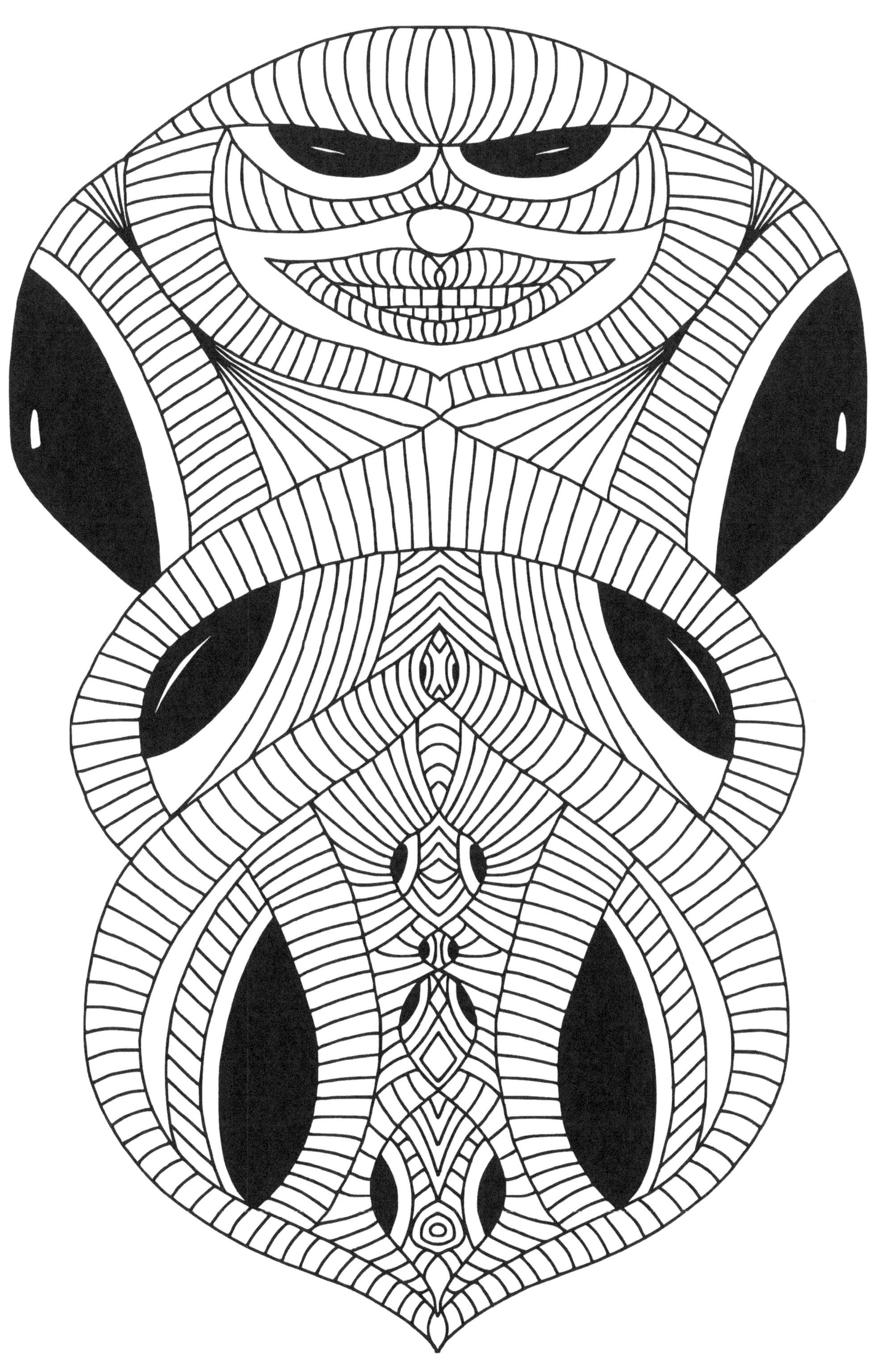

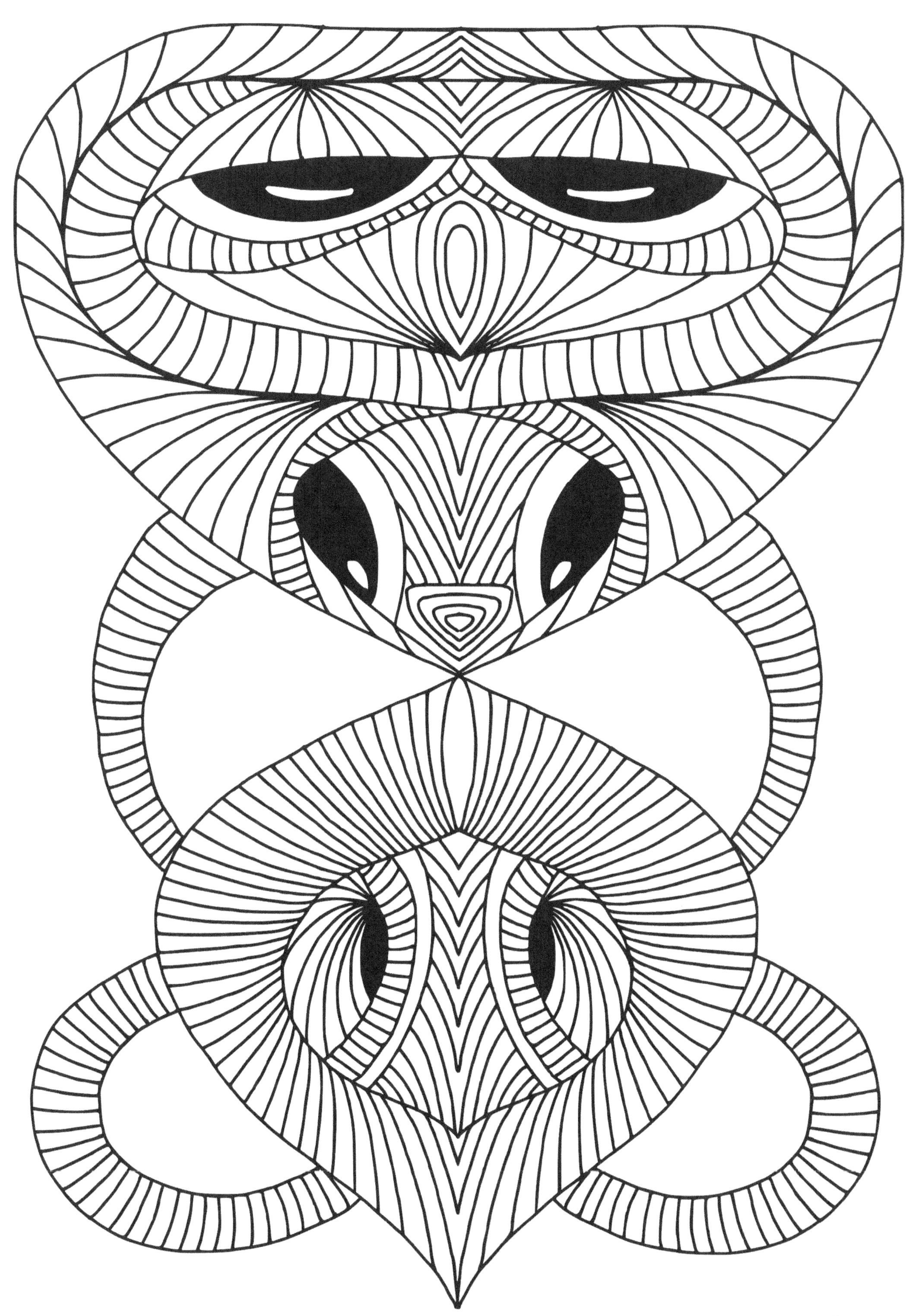

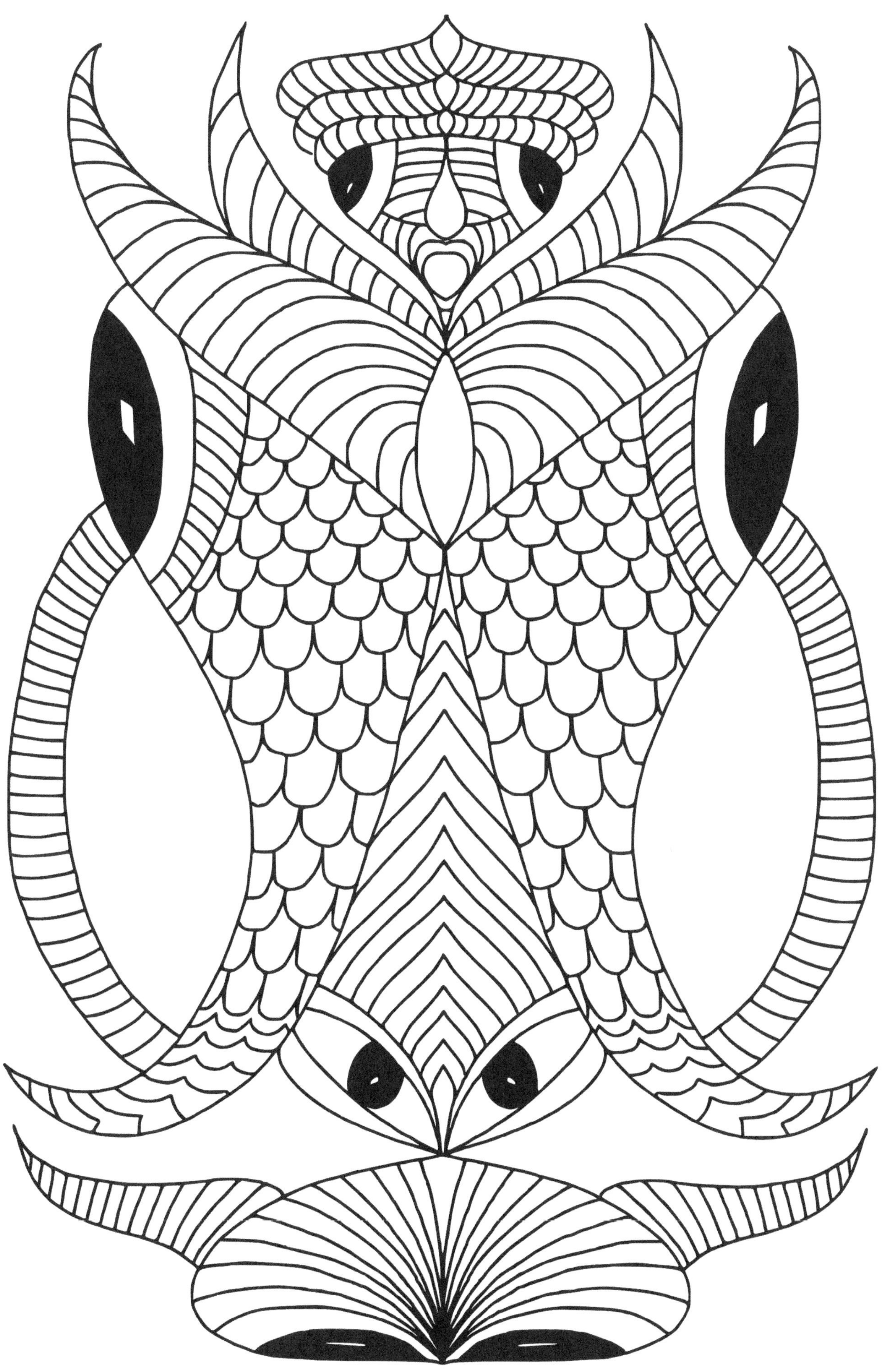

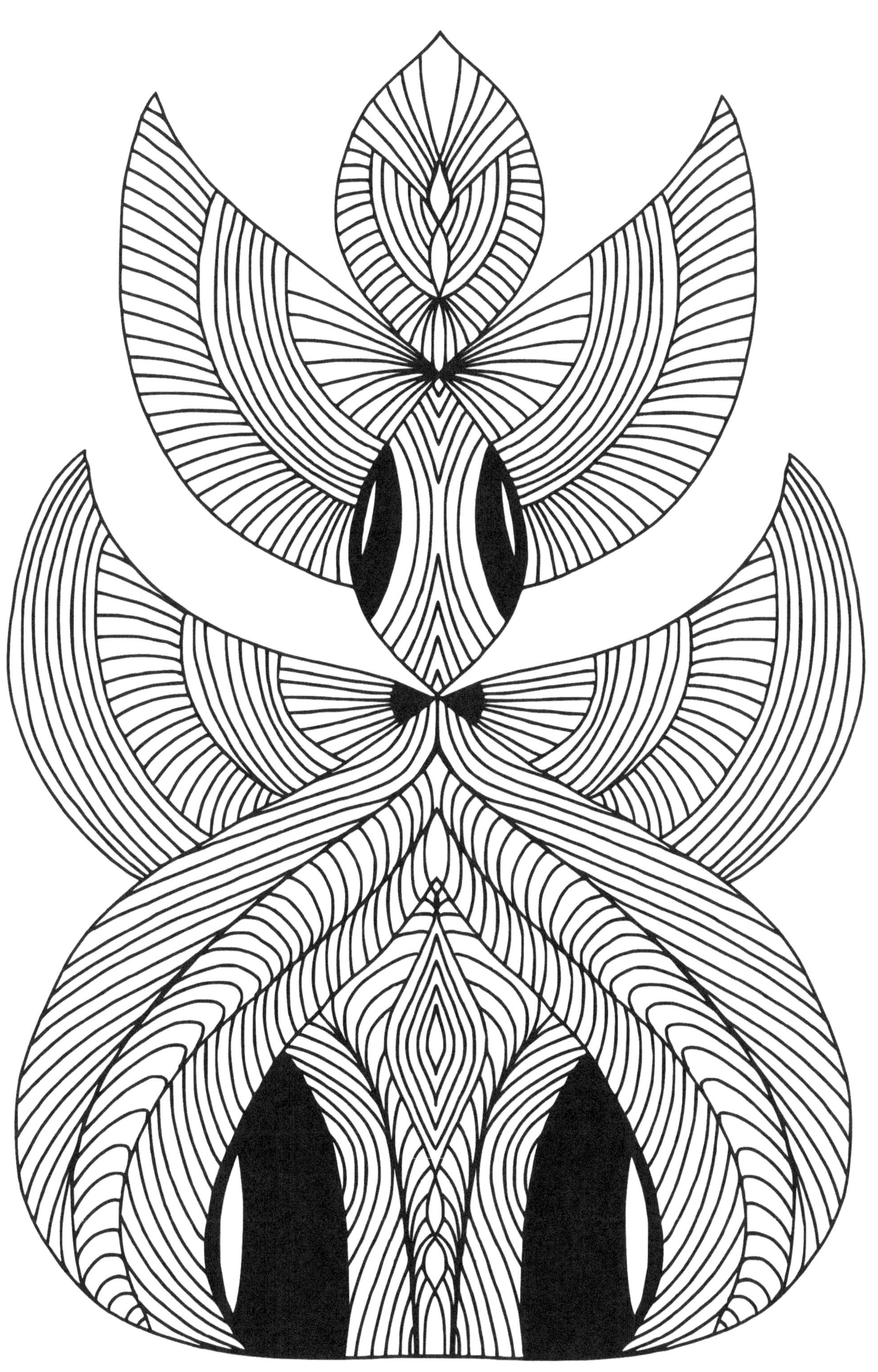

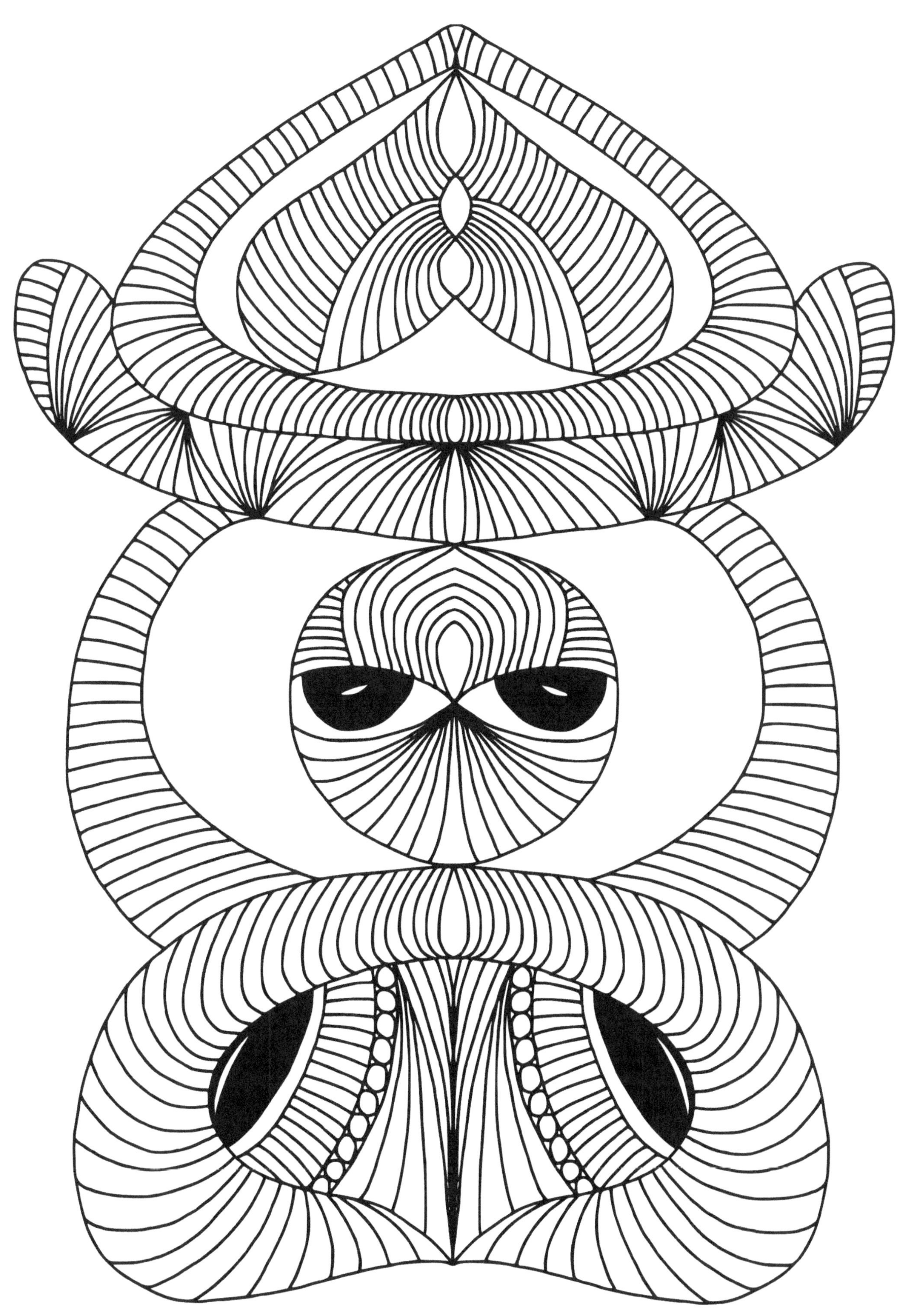

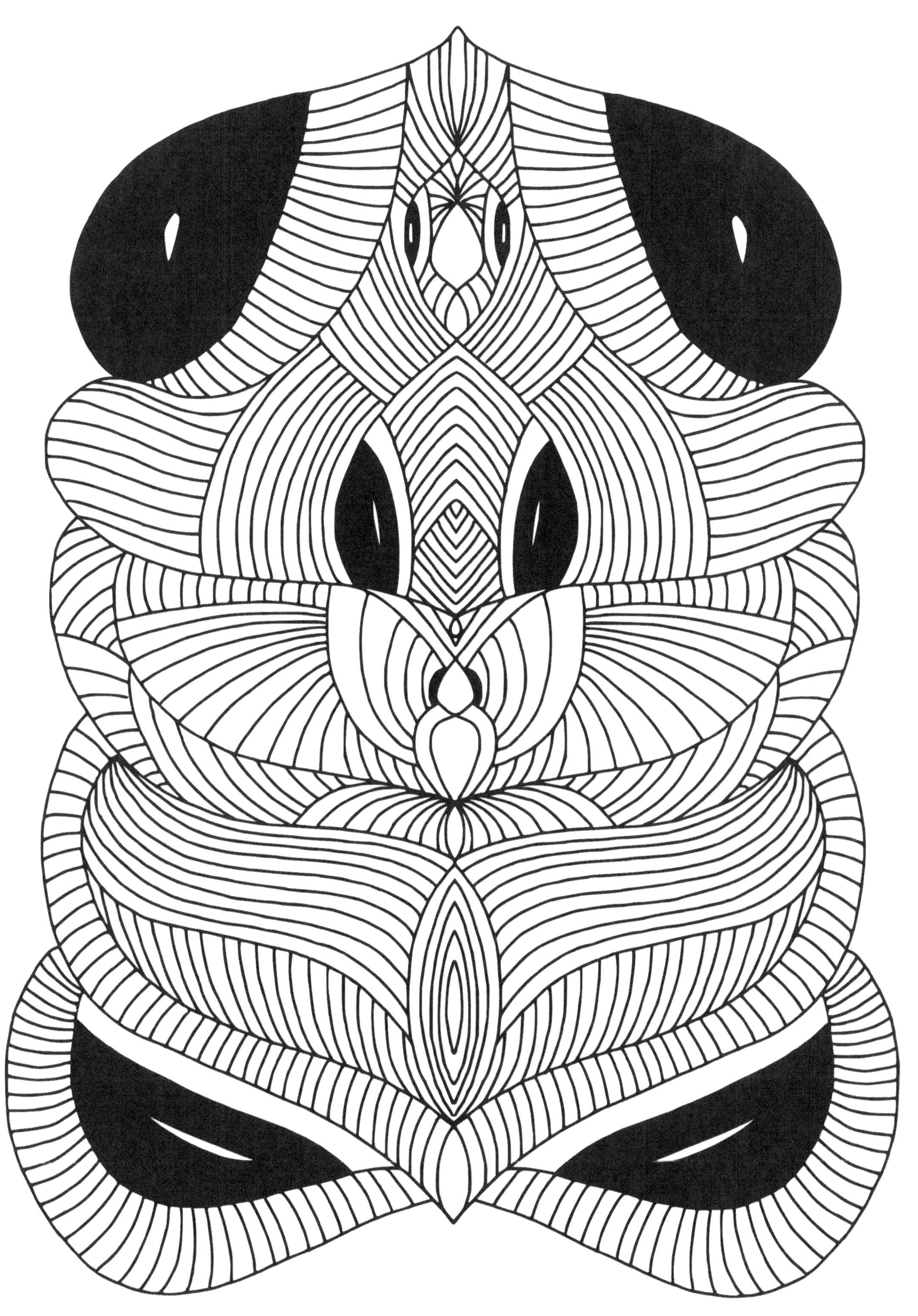

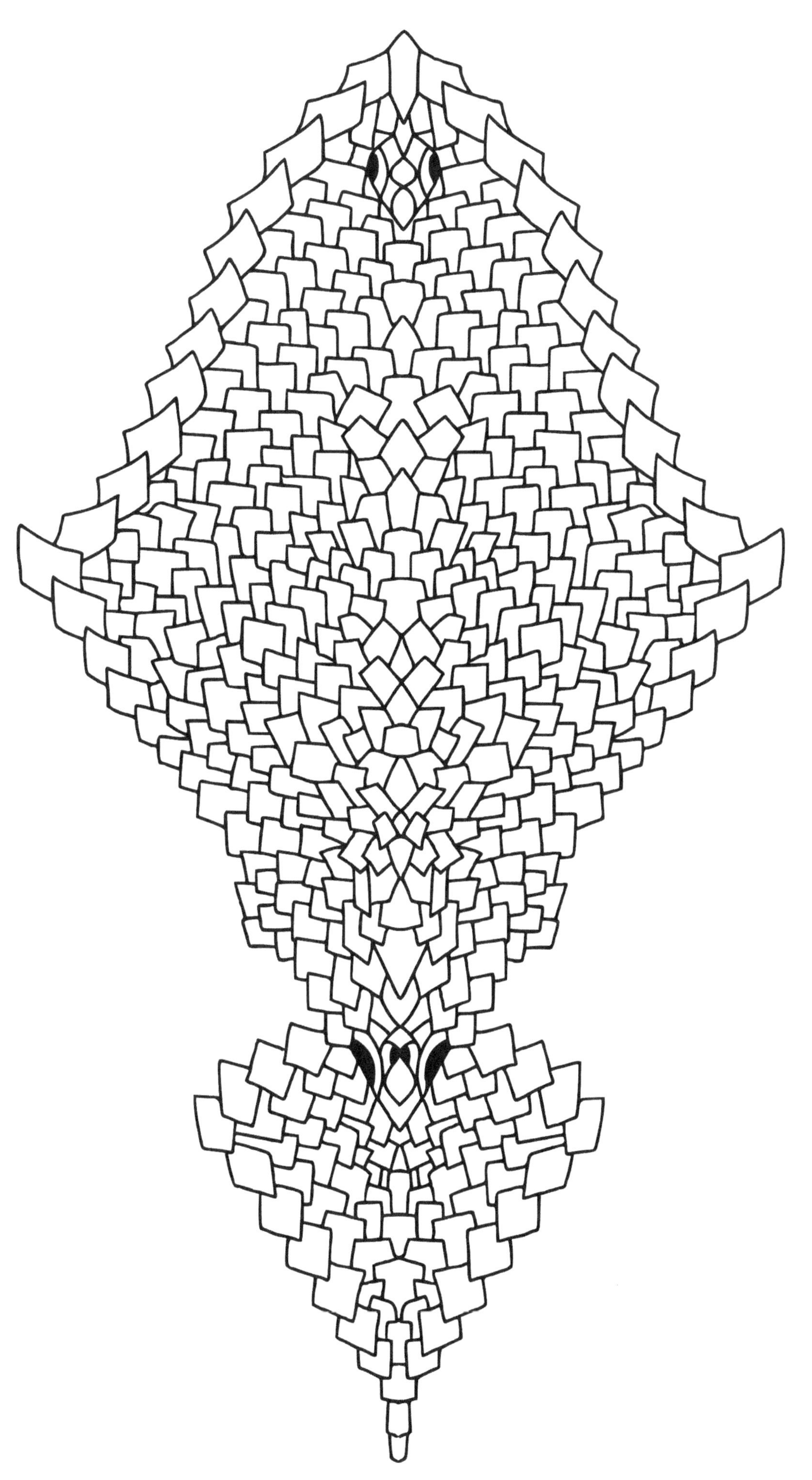

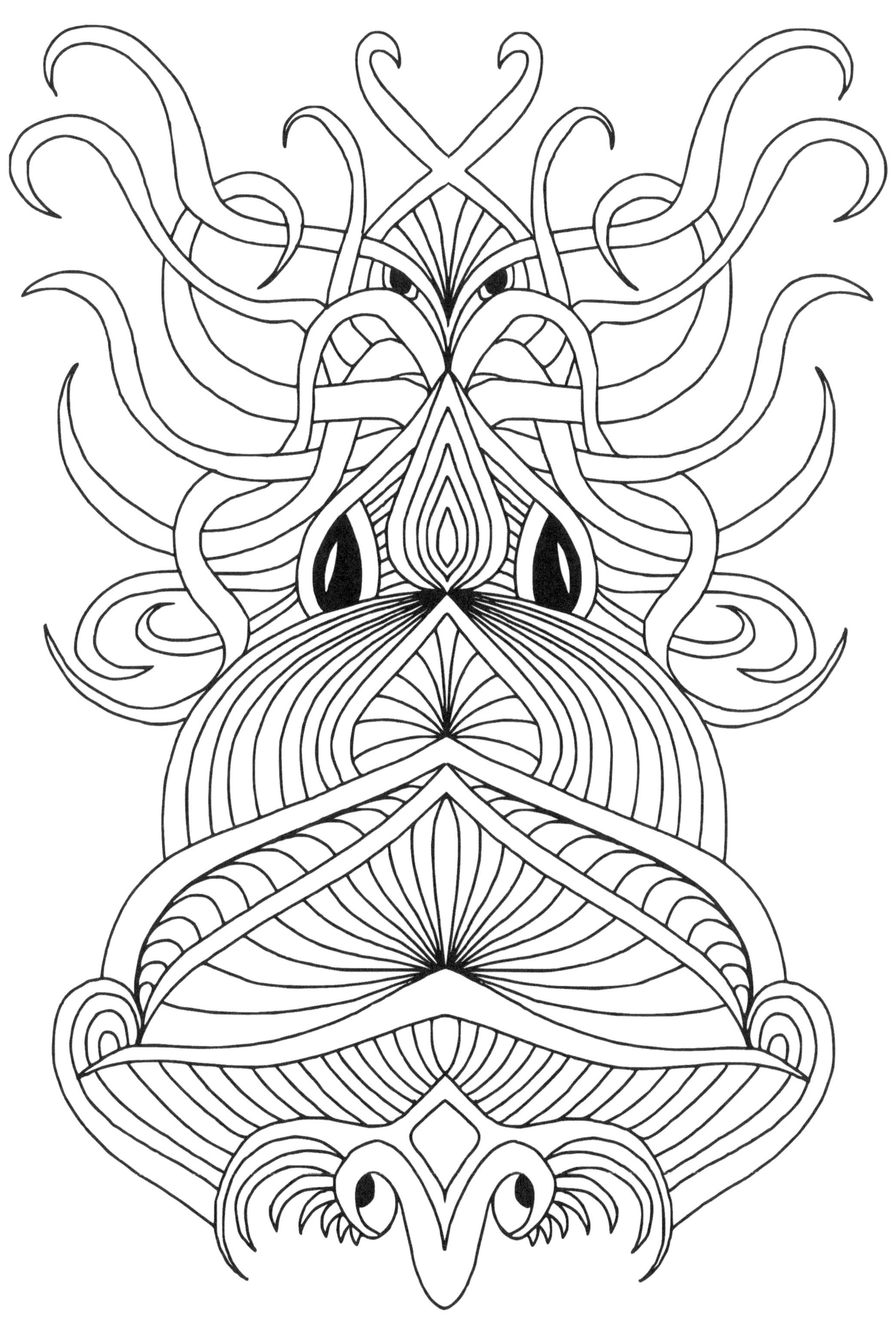

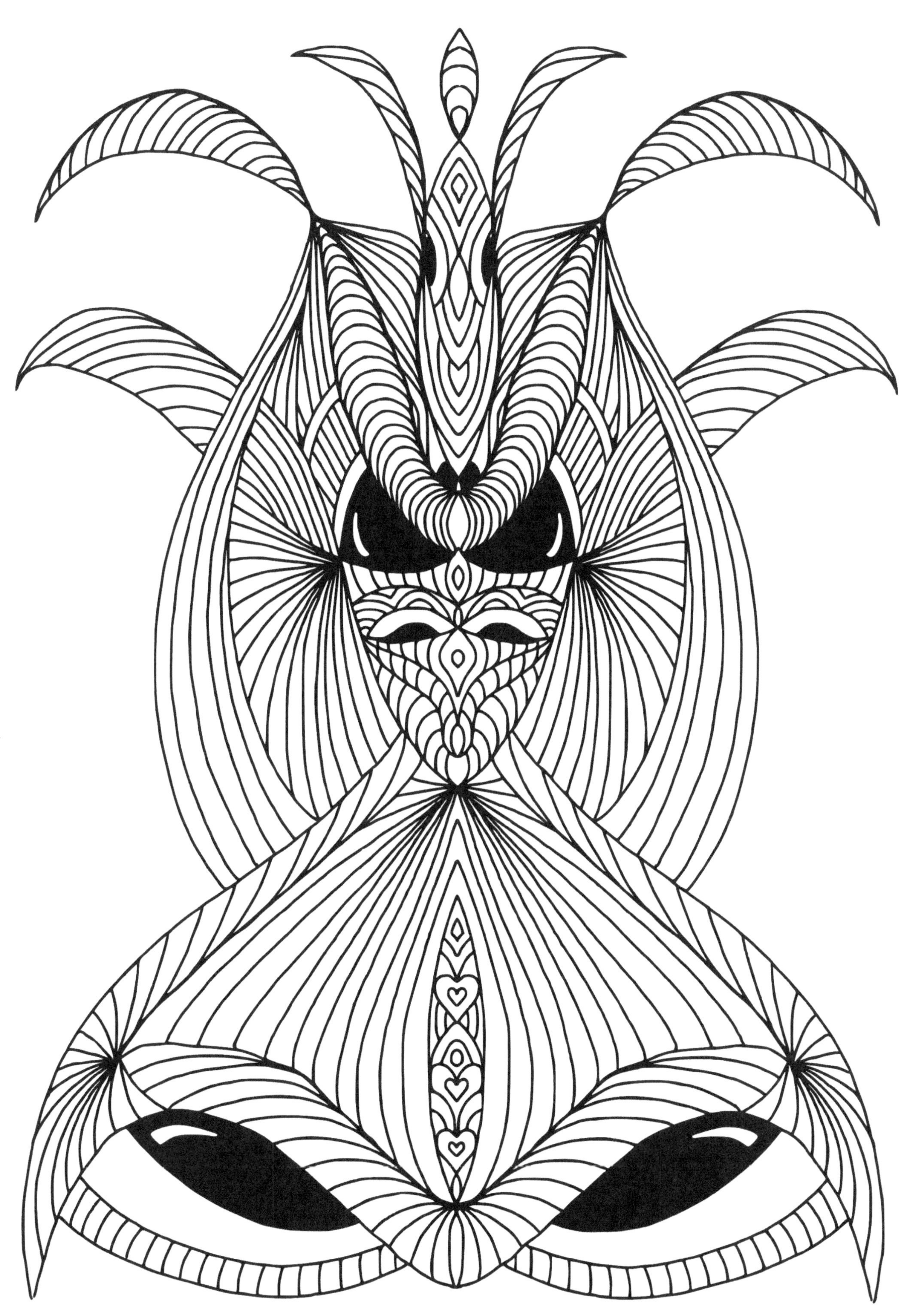

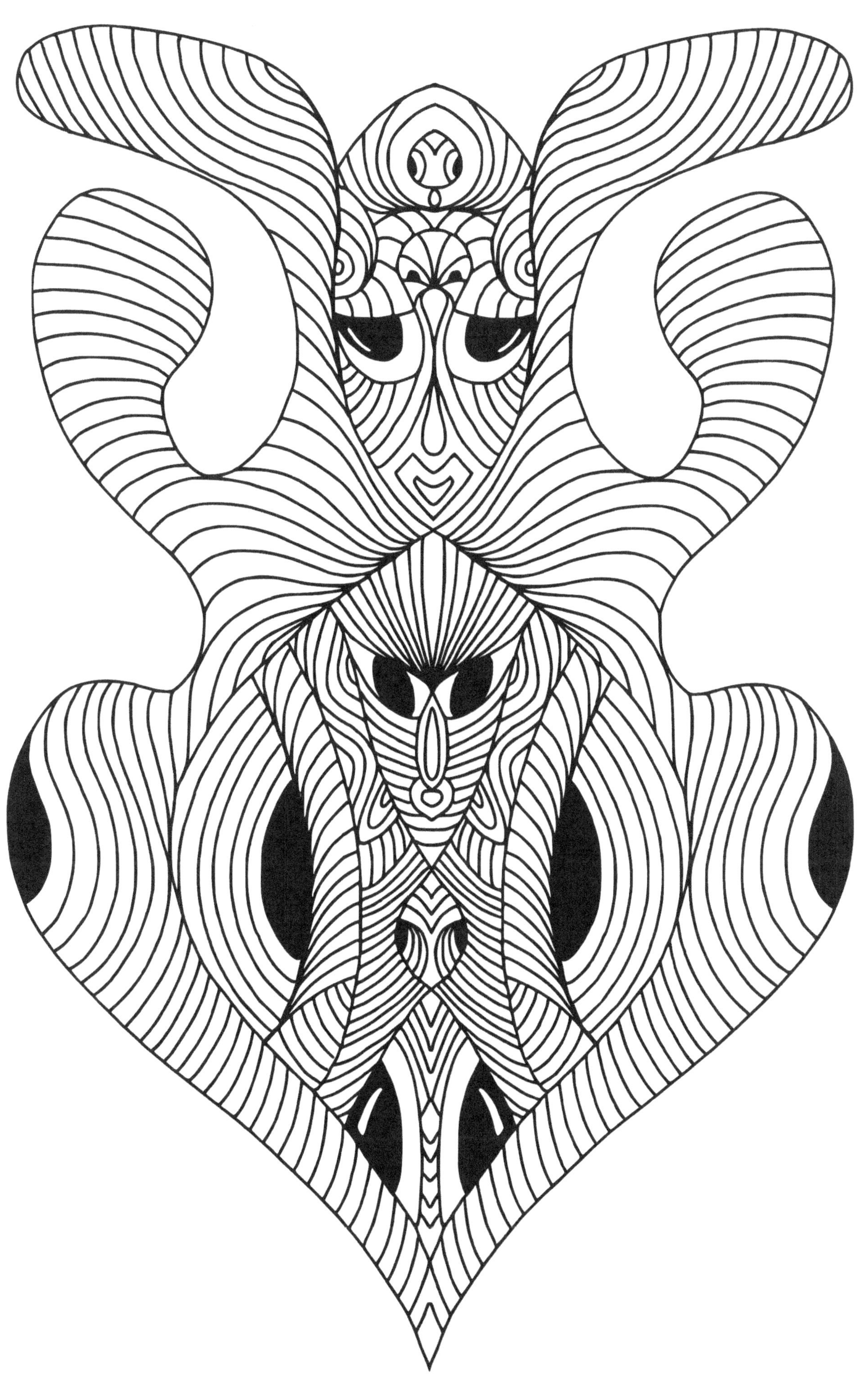

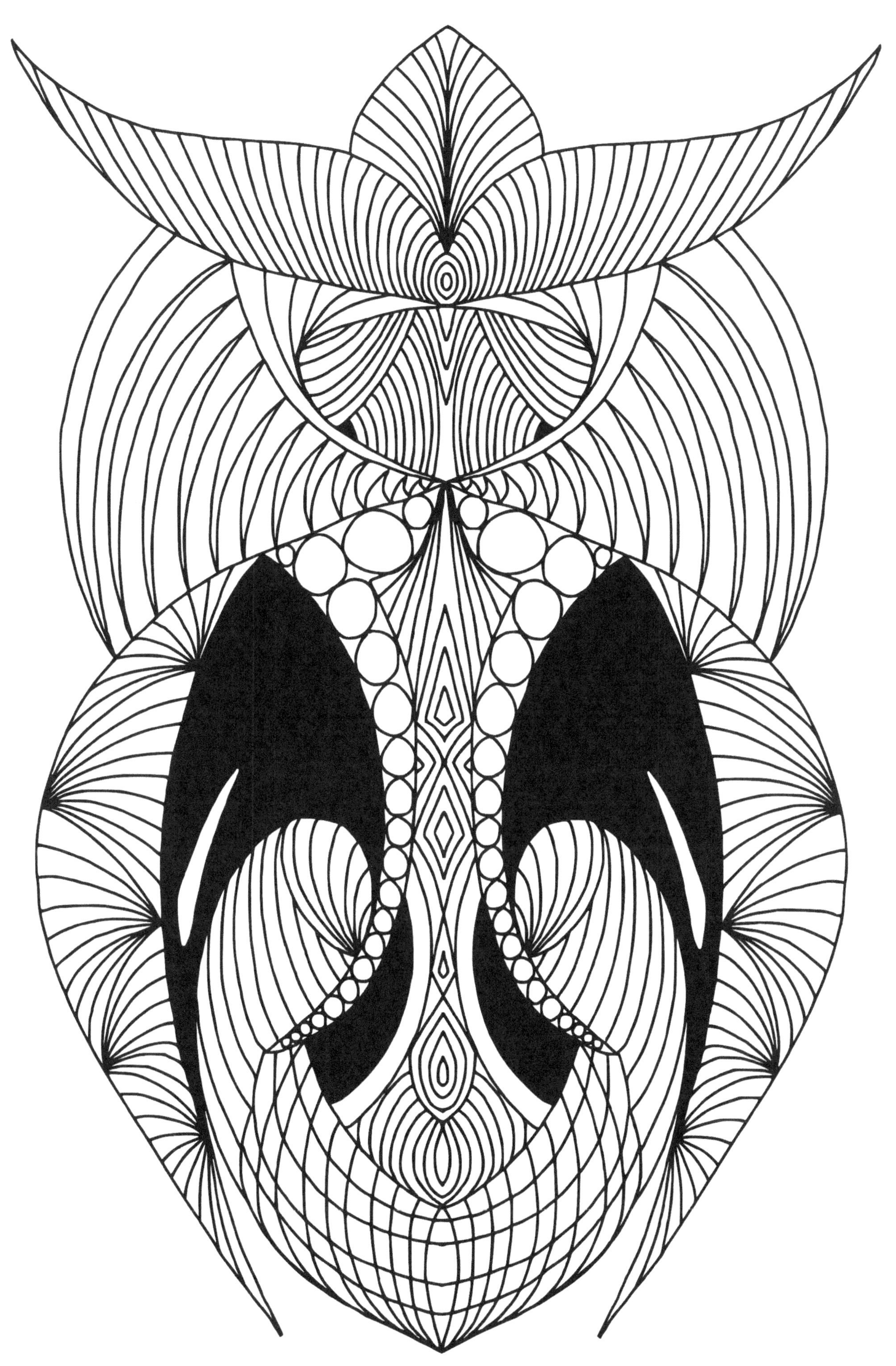

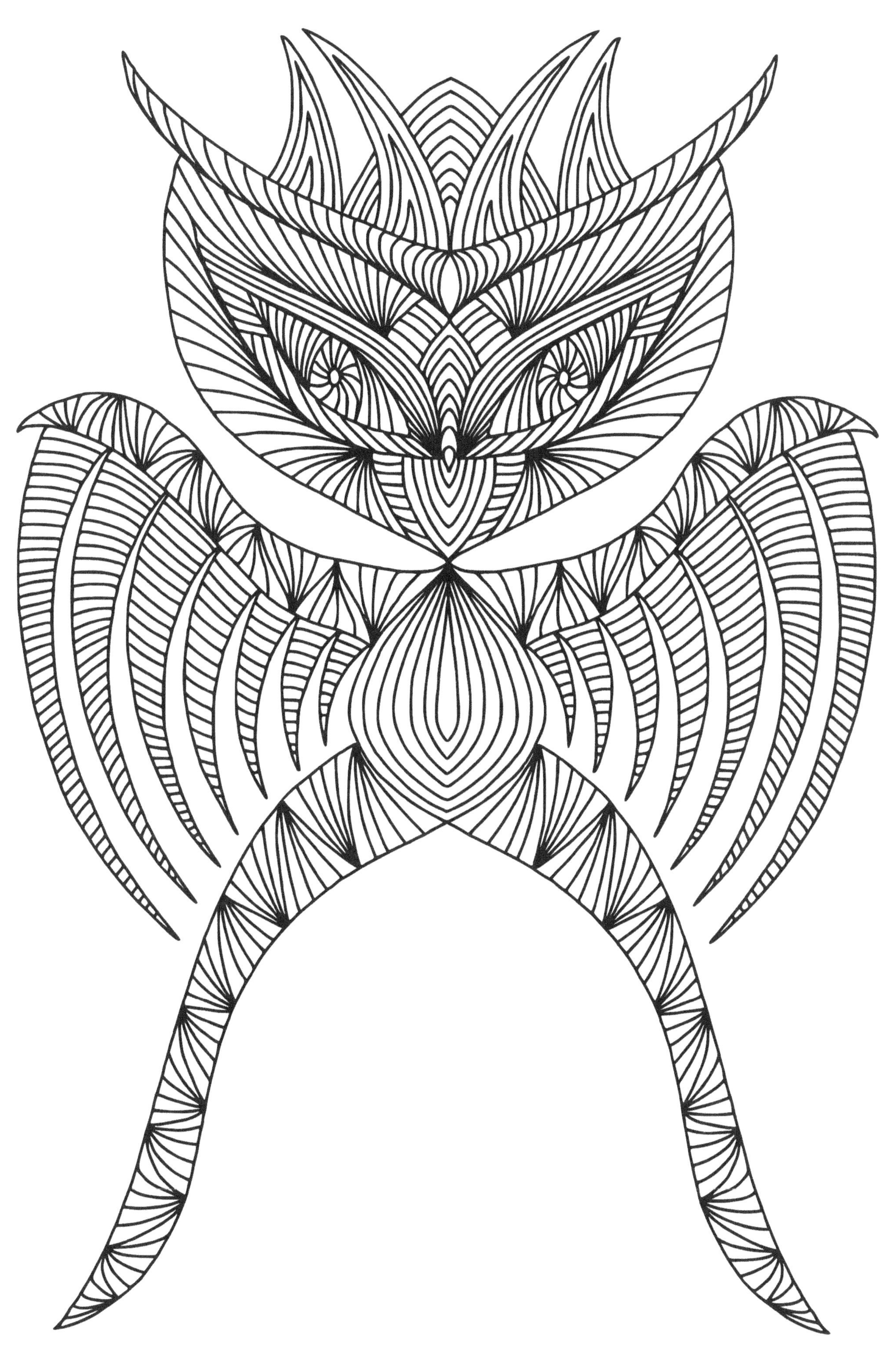

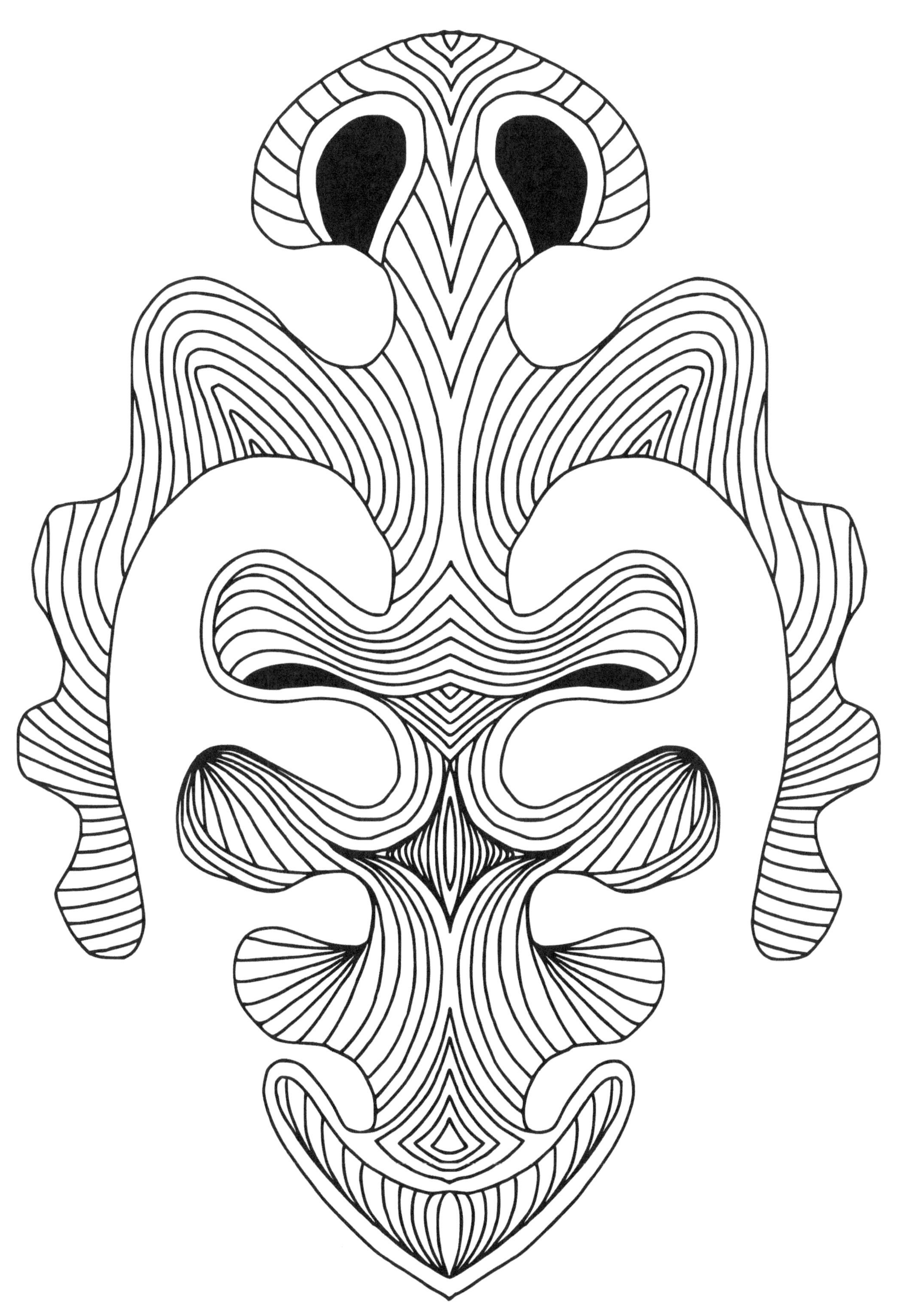

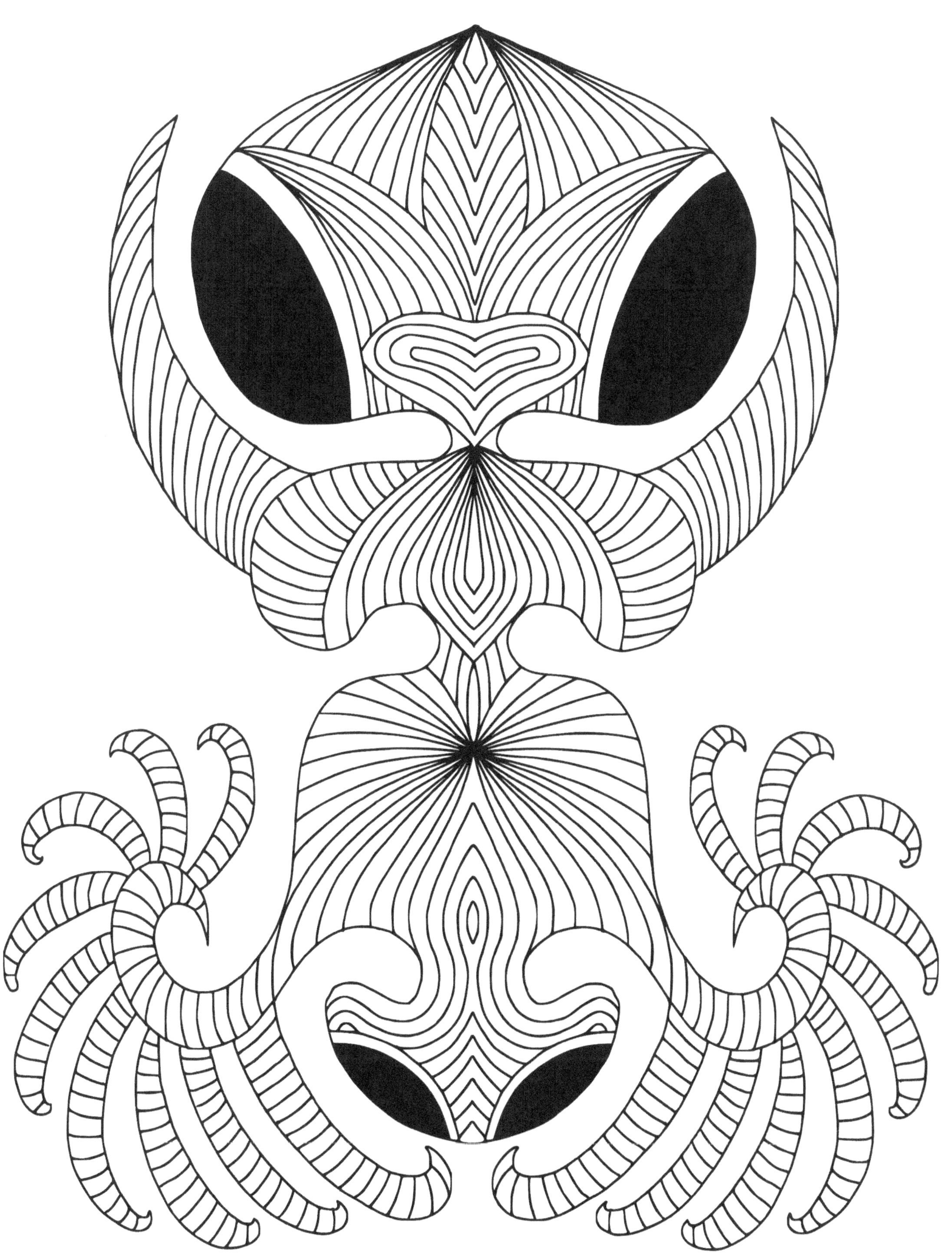

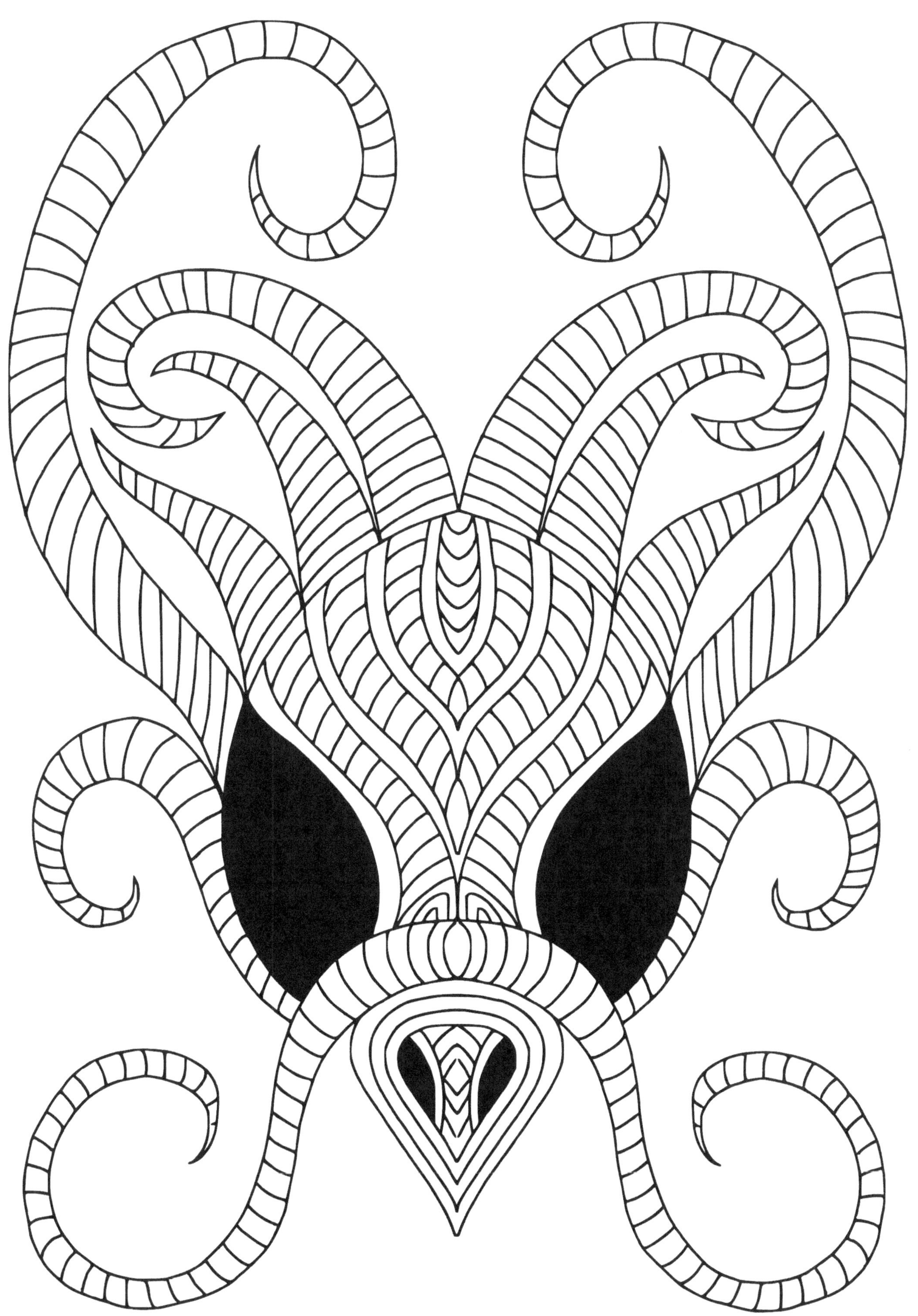

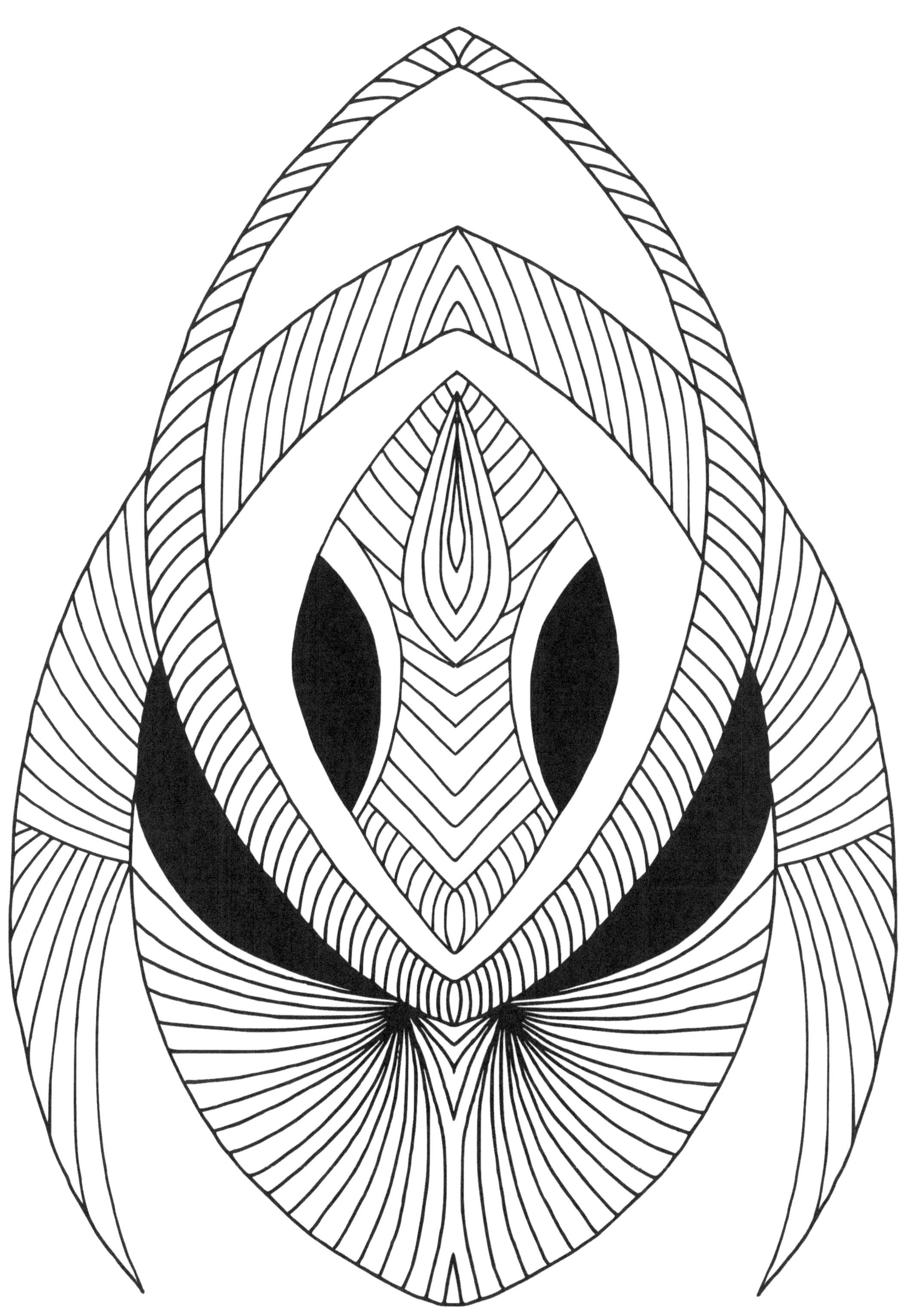

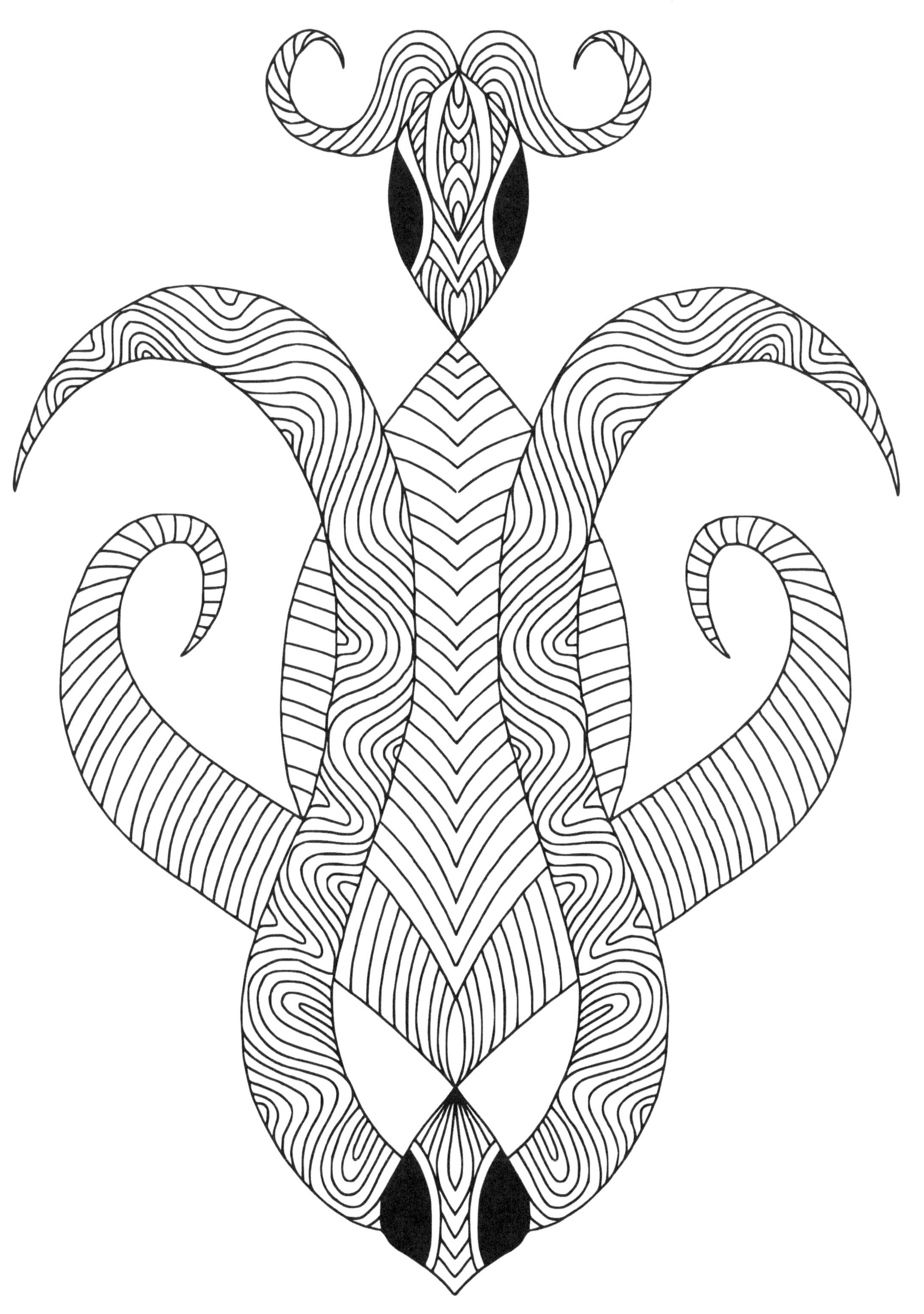

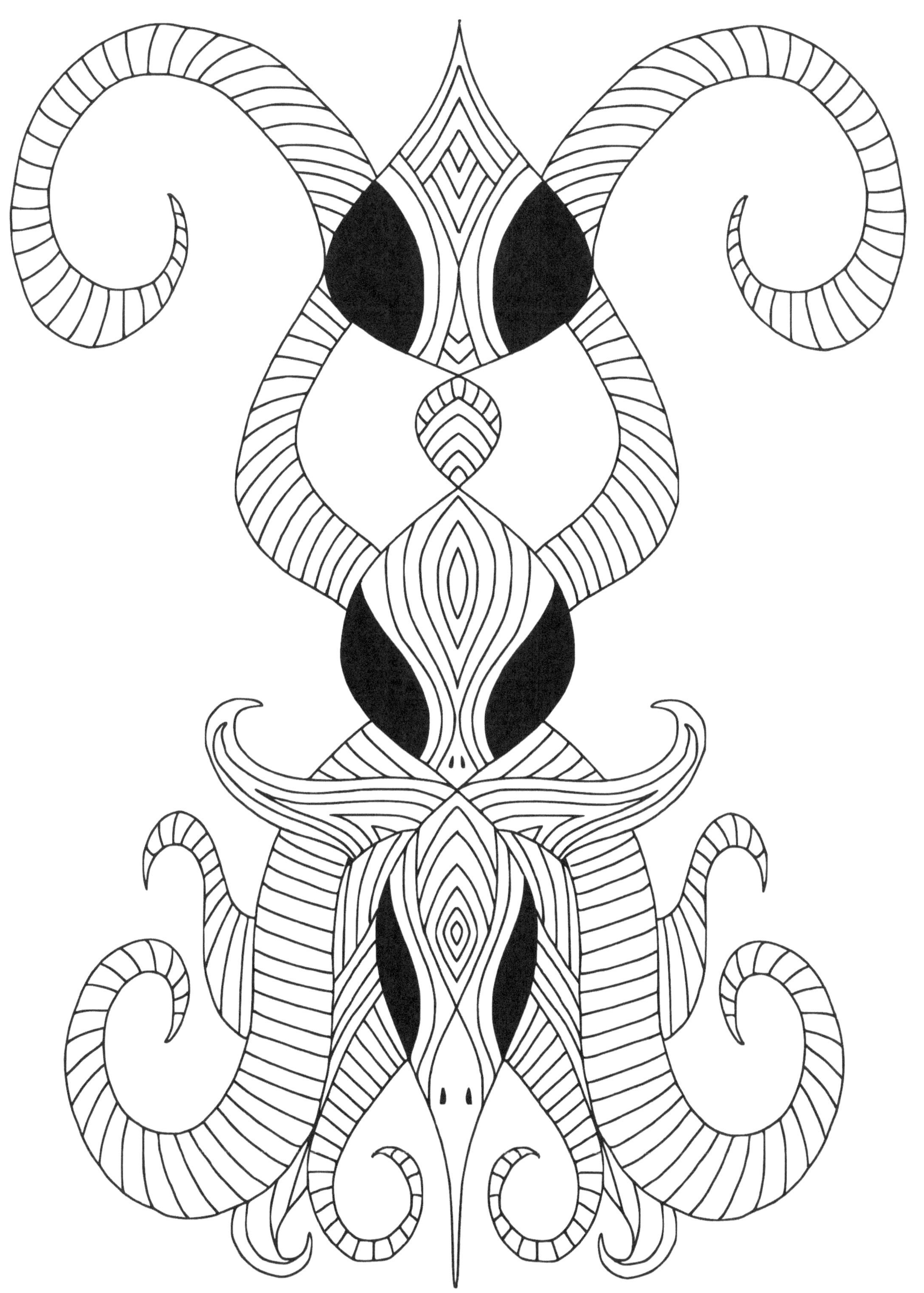

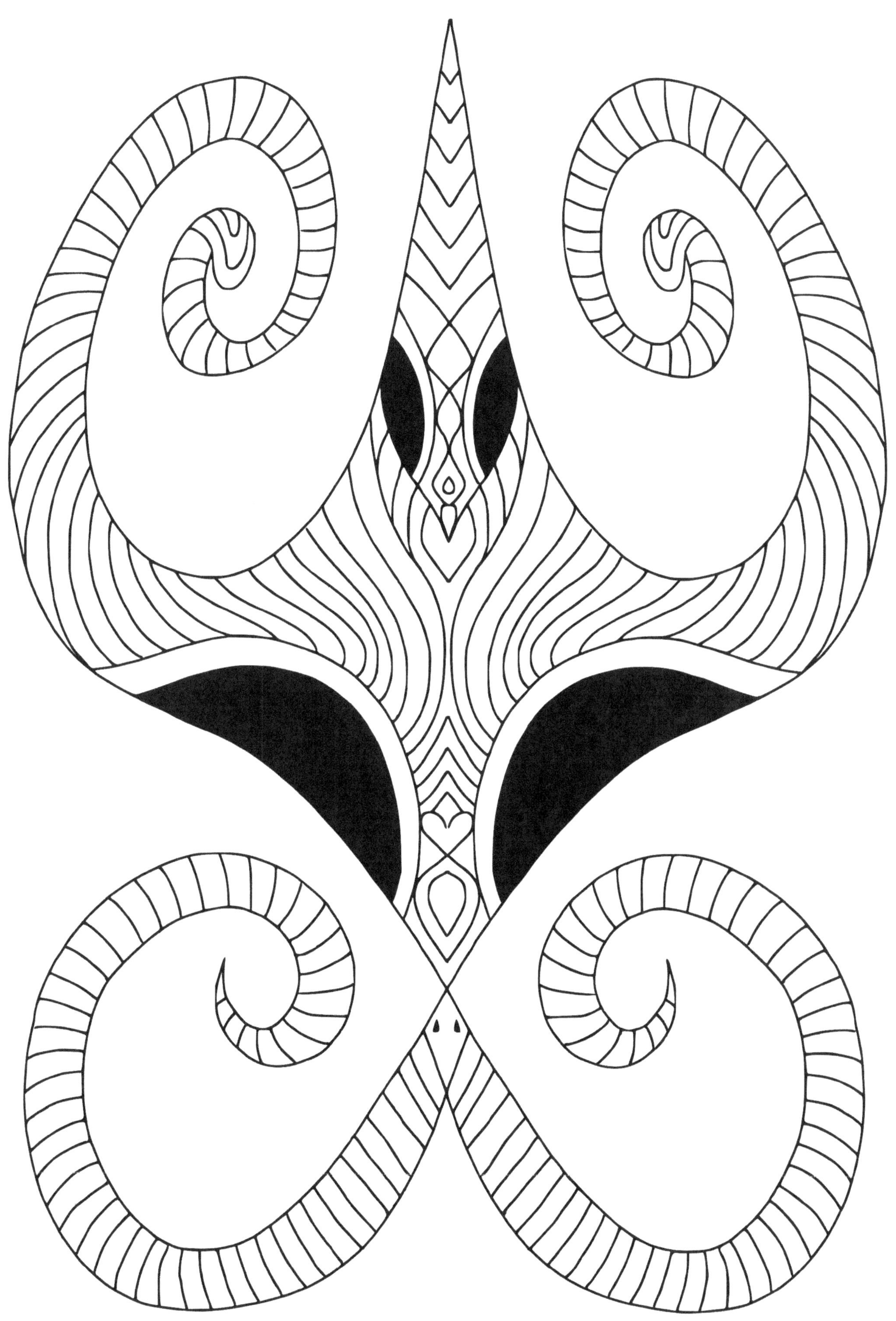

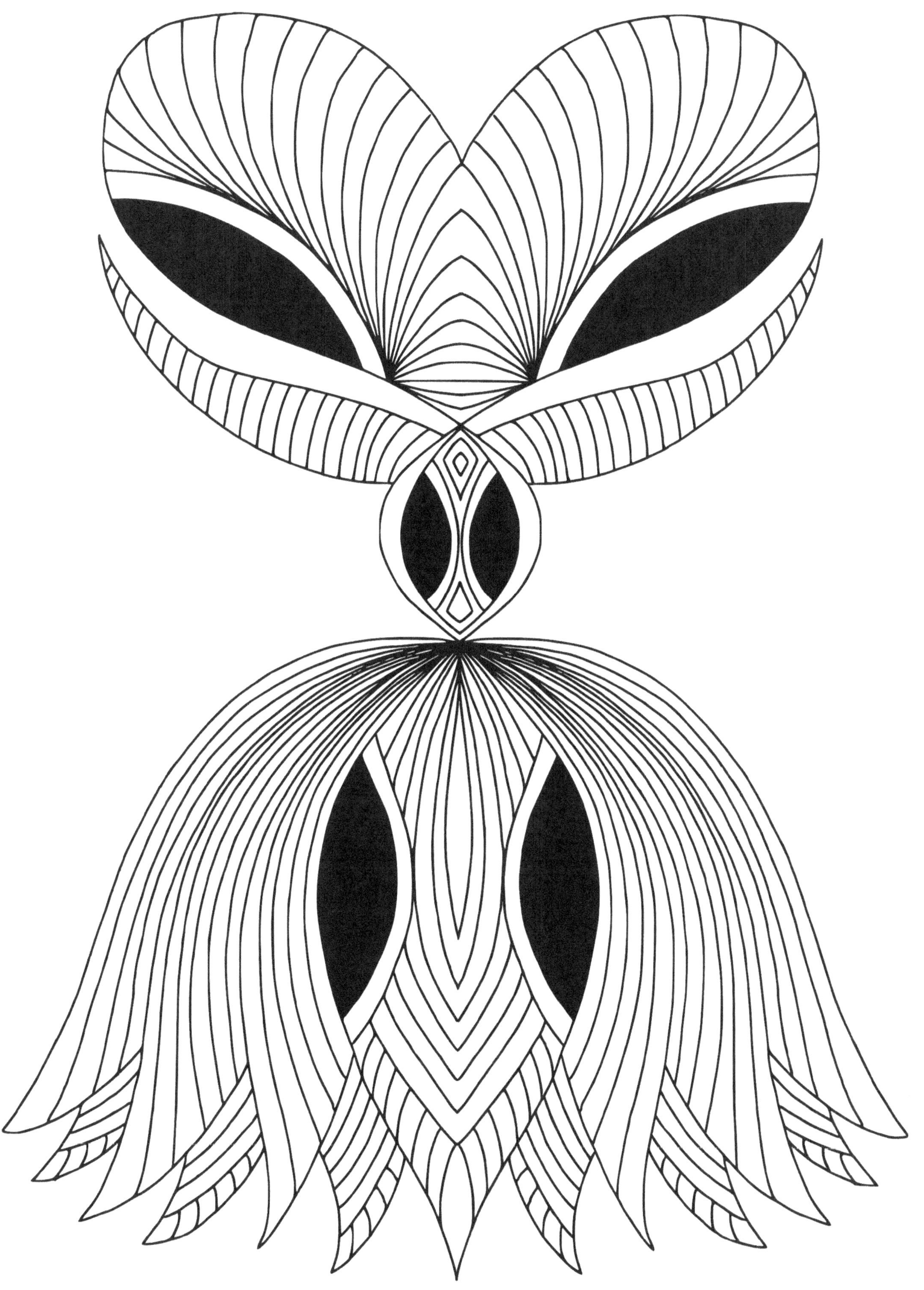

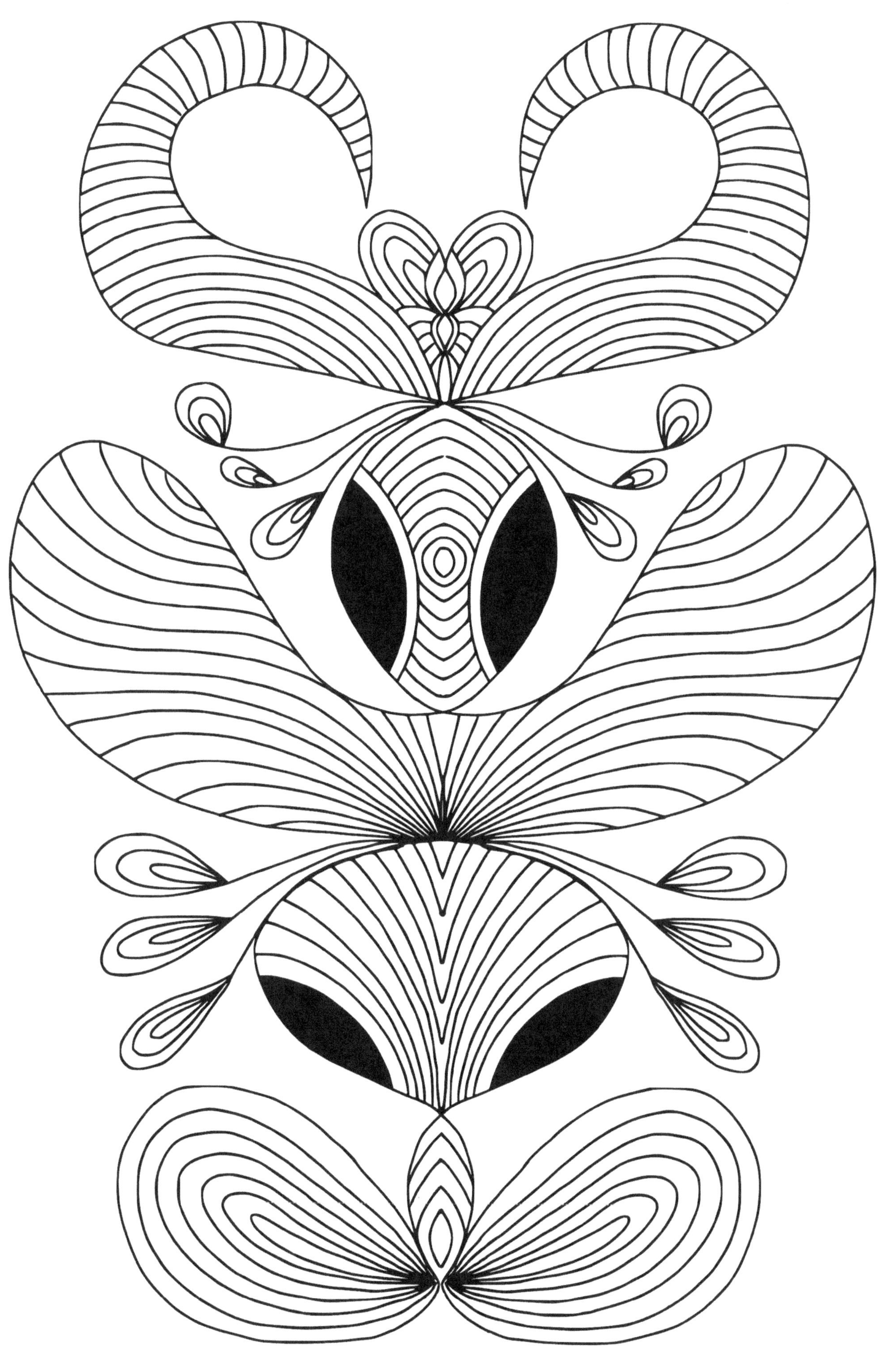

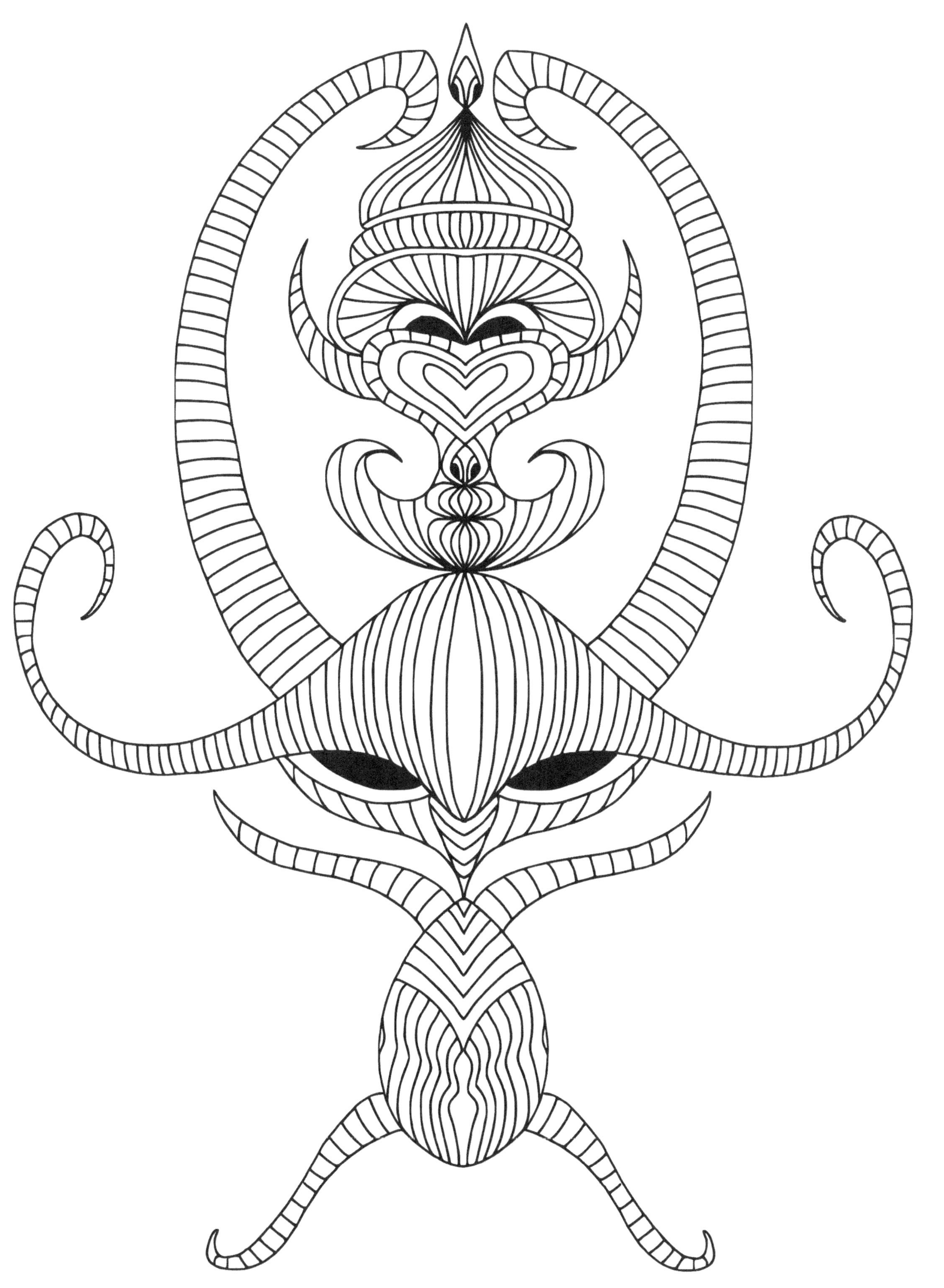

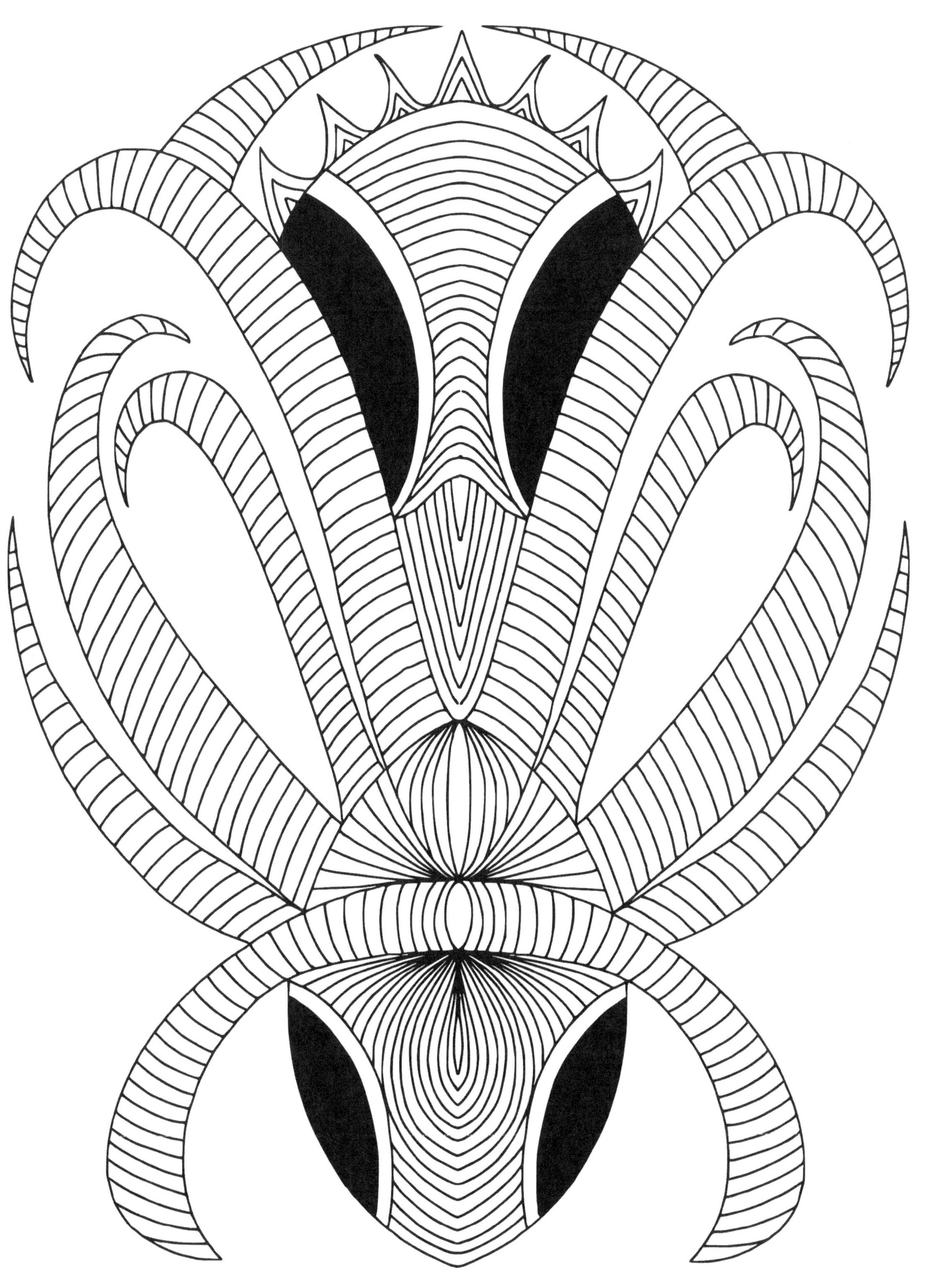

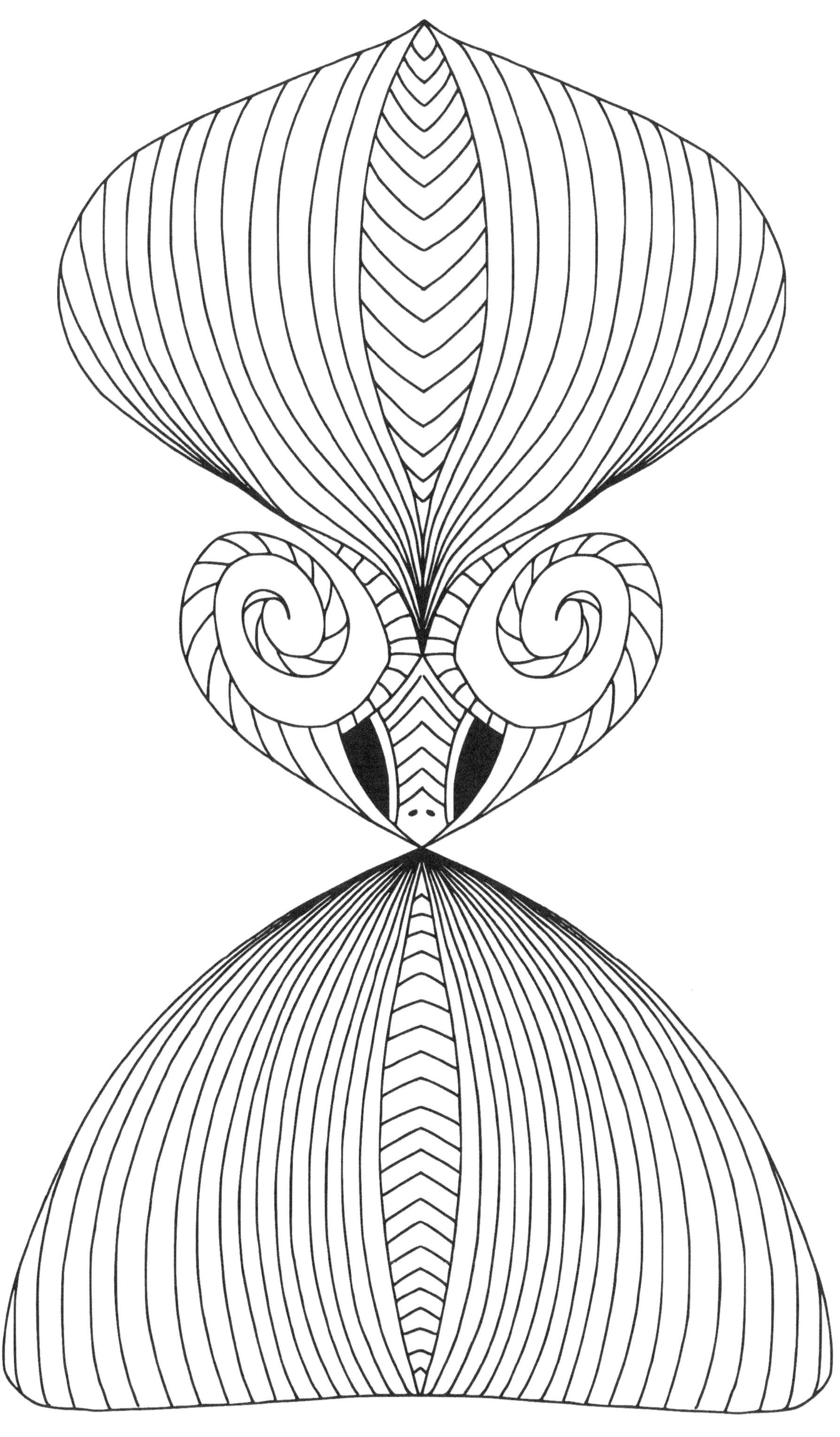

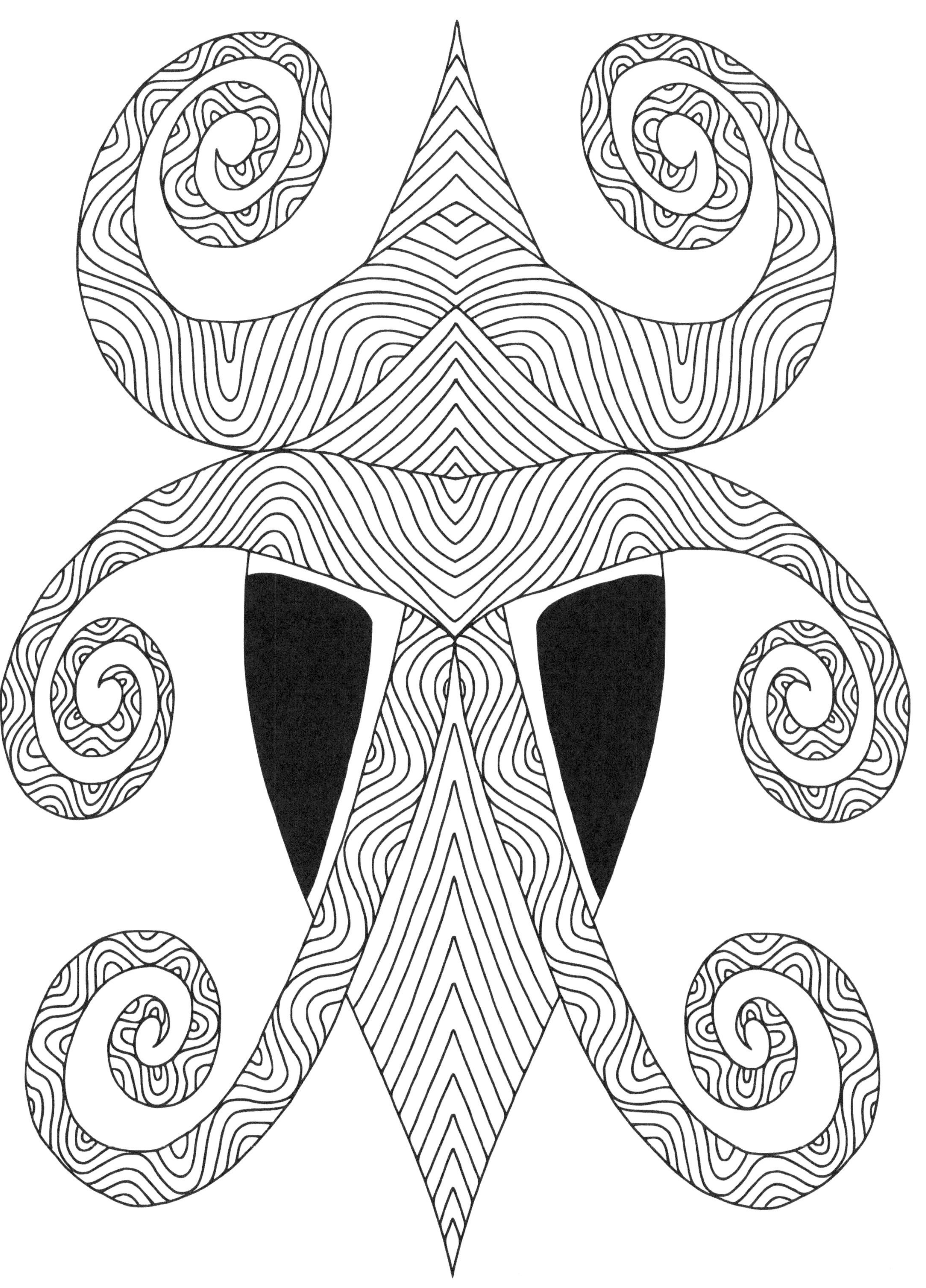

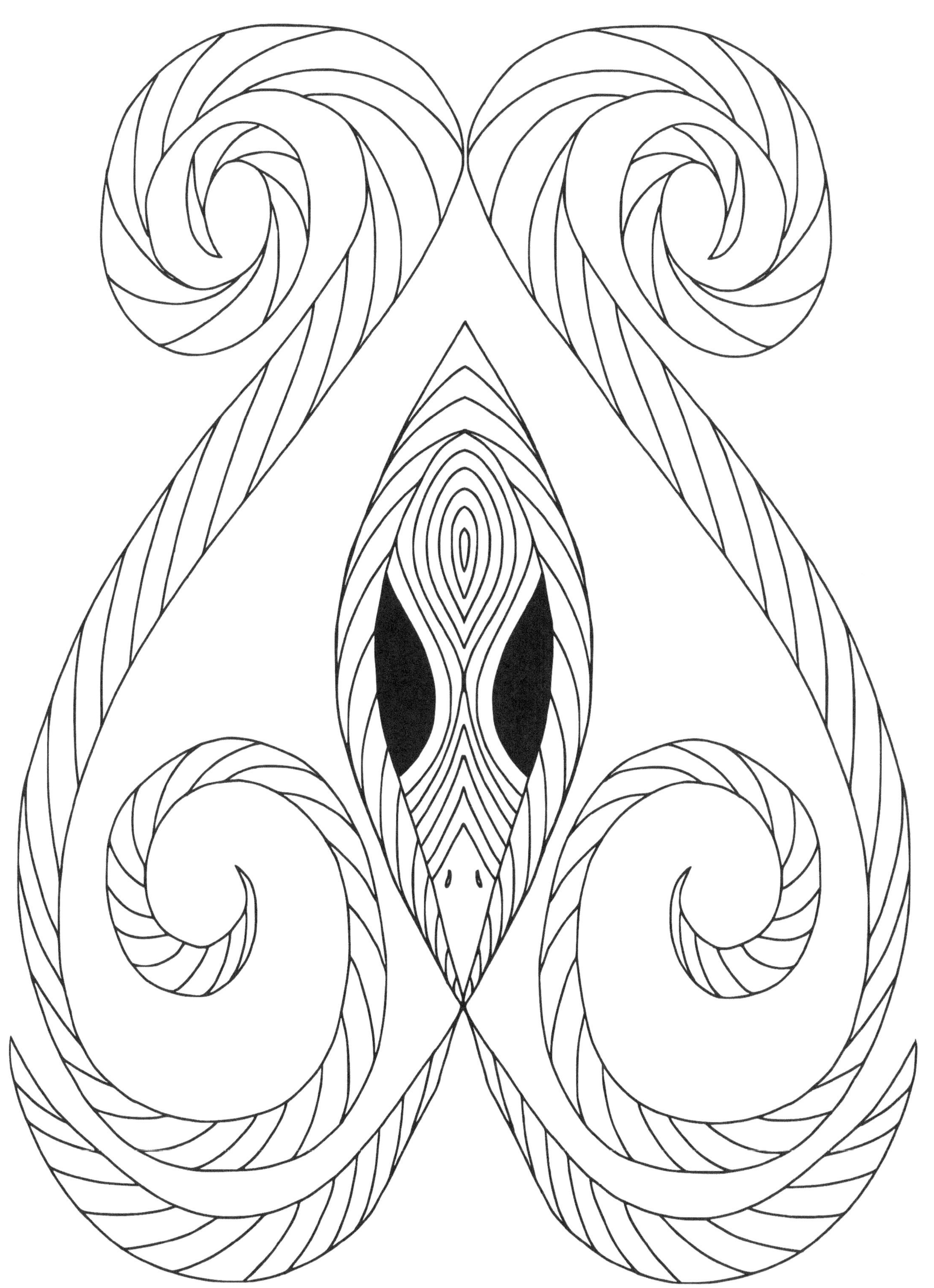

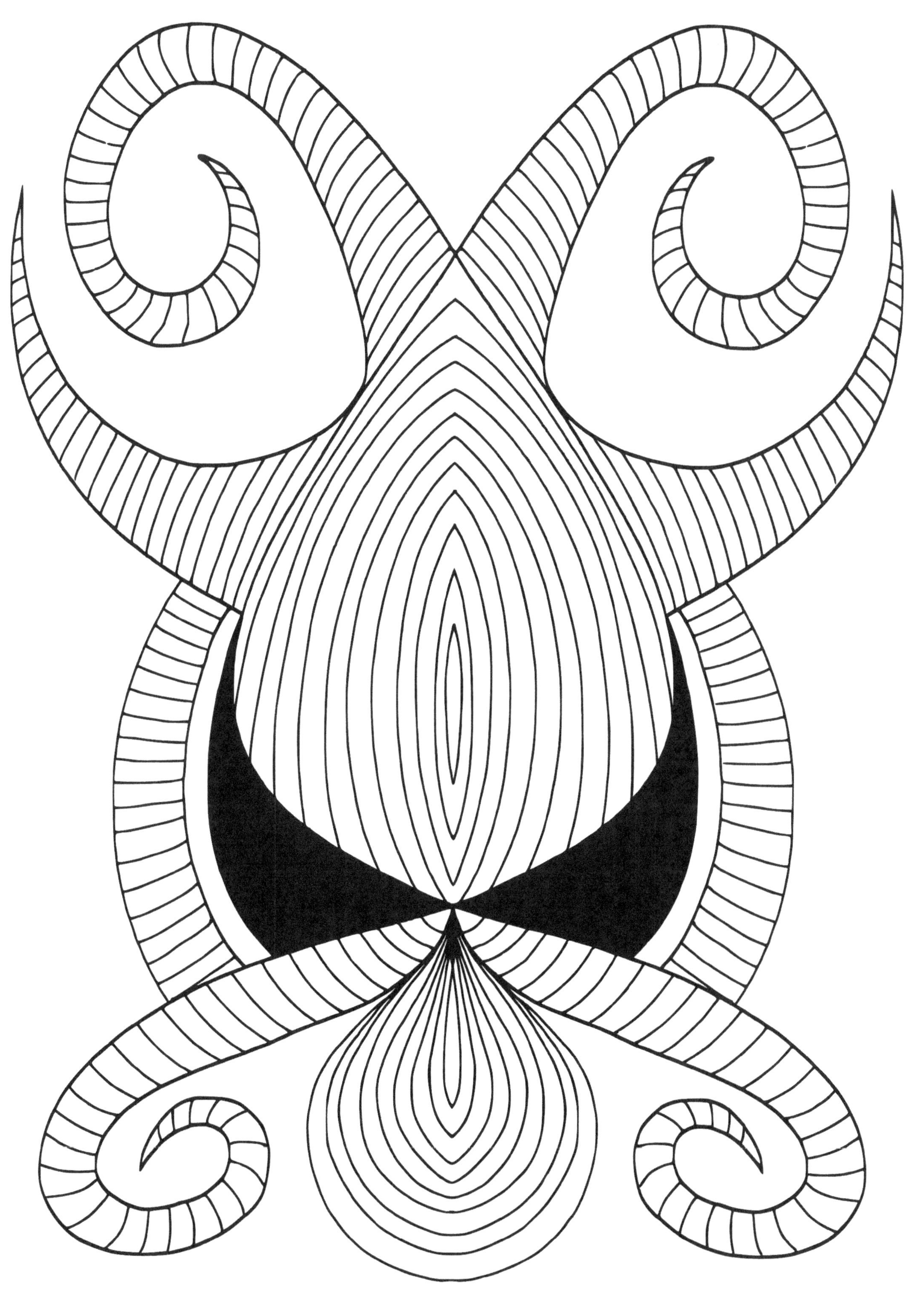

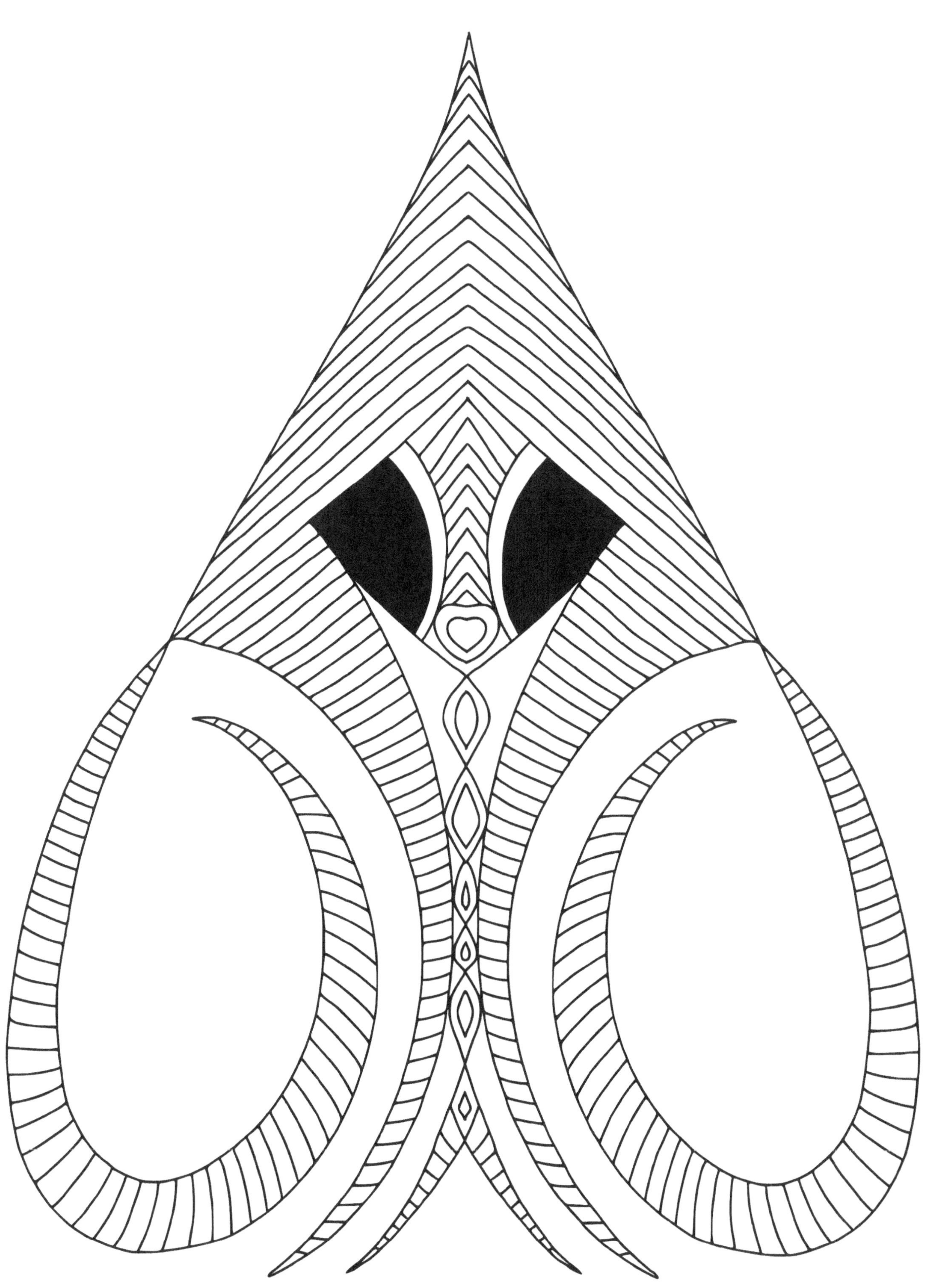

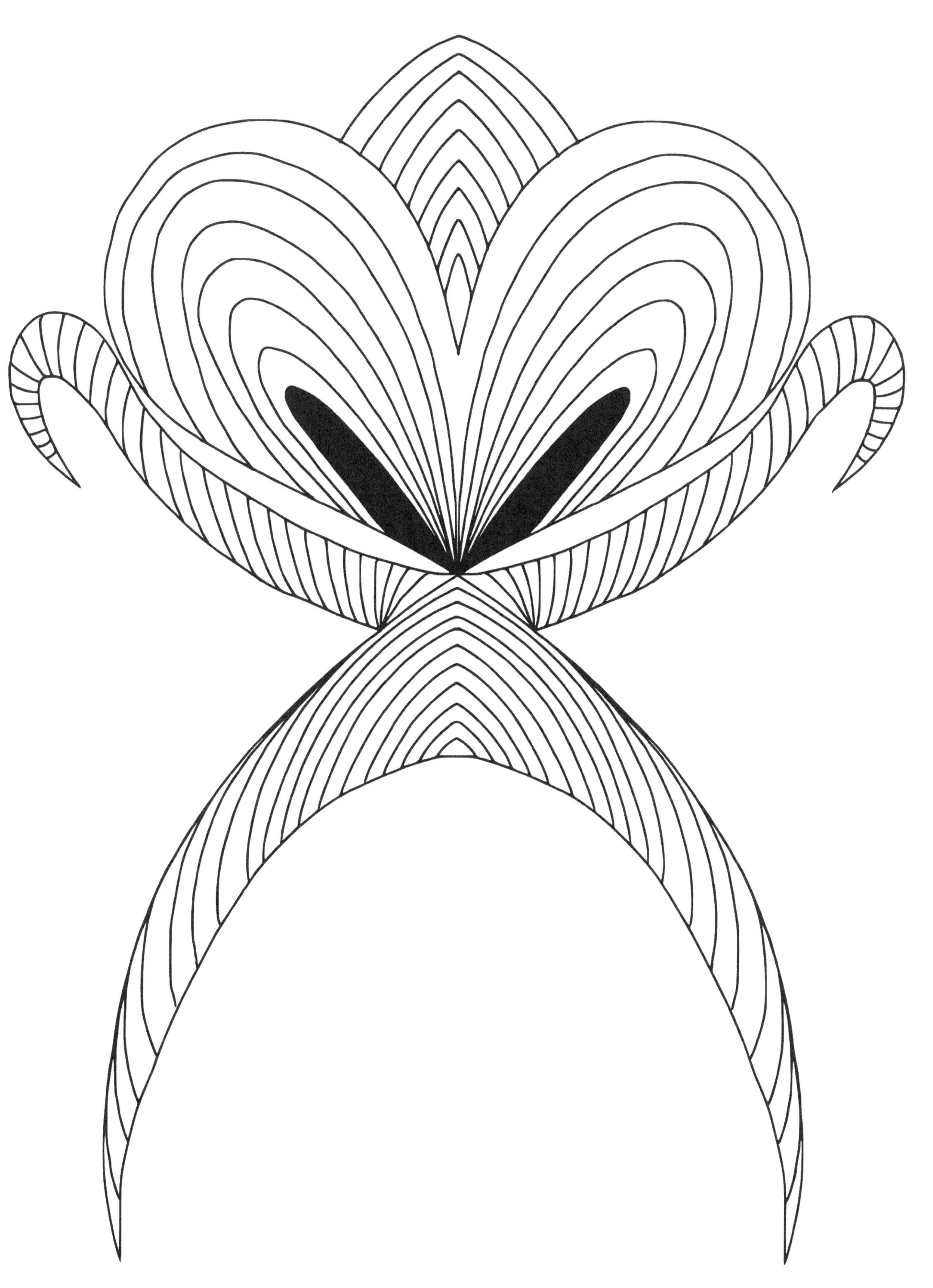

Bonus Upside Down versions......

Bonus Upside Down versions......

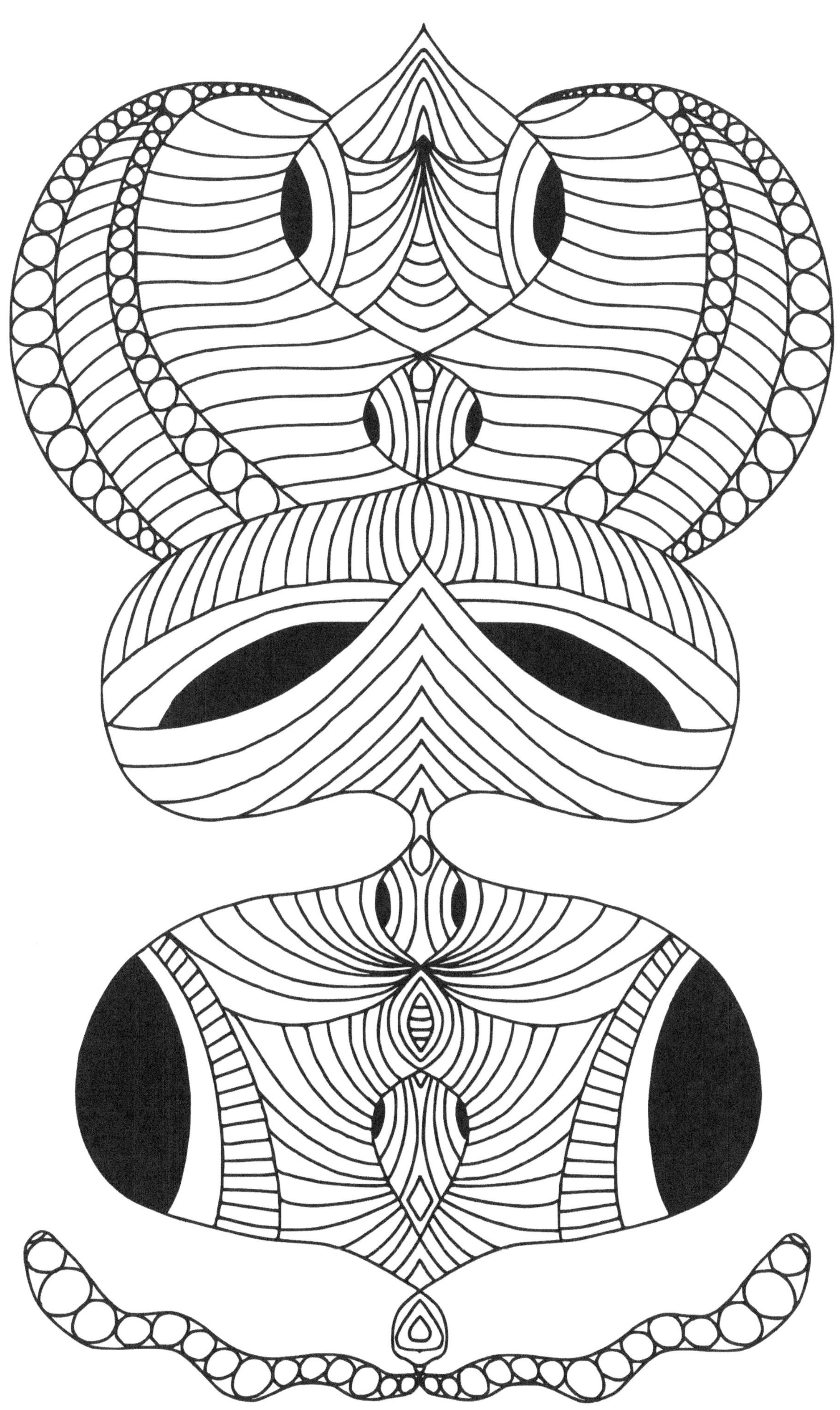

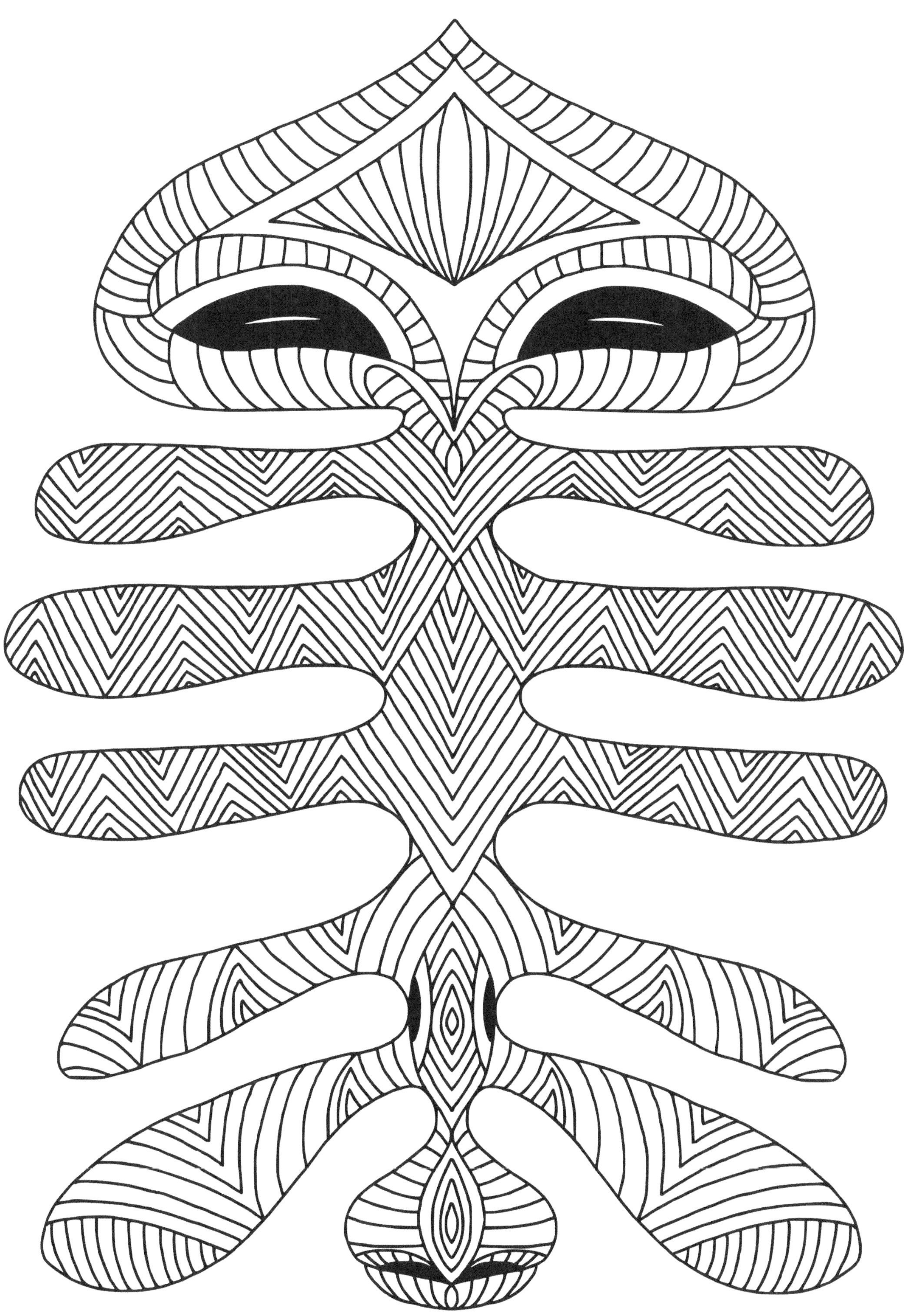

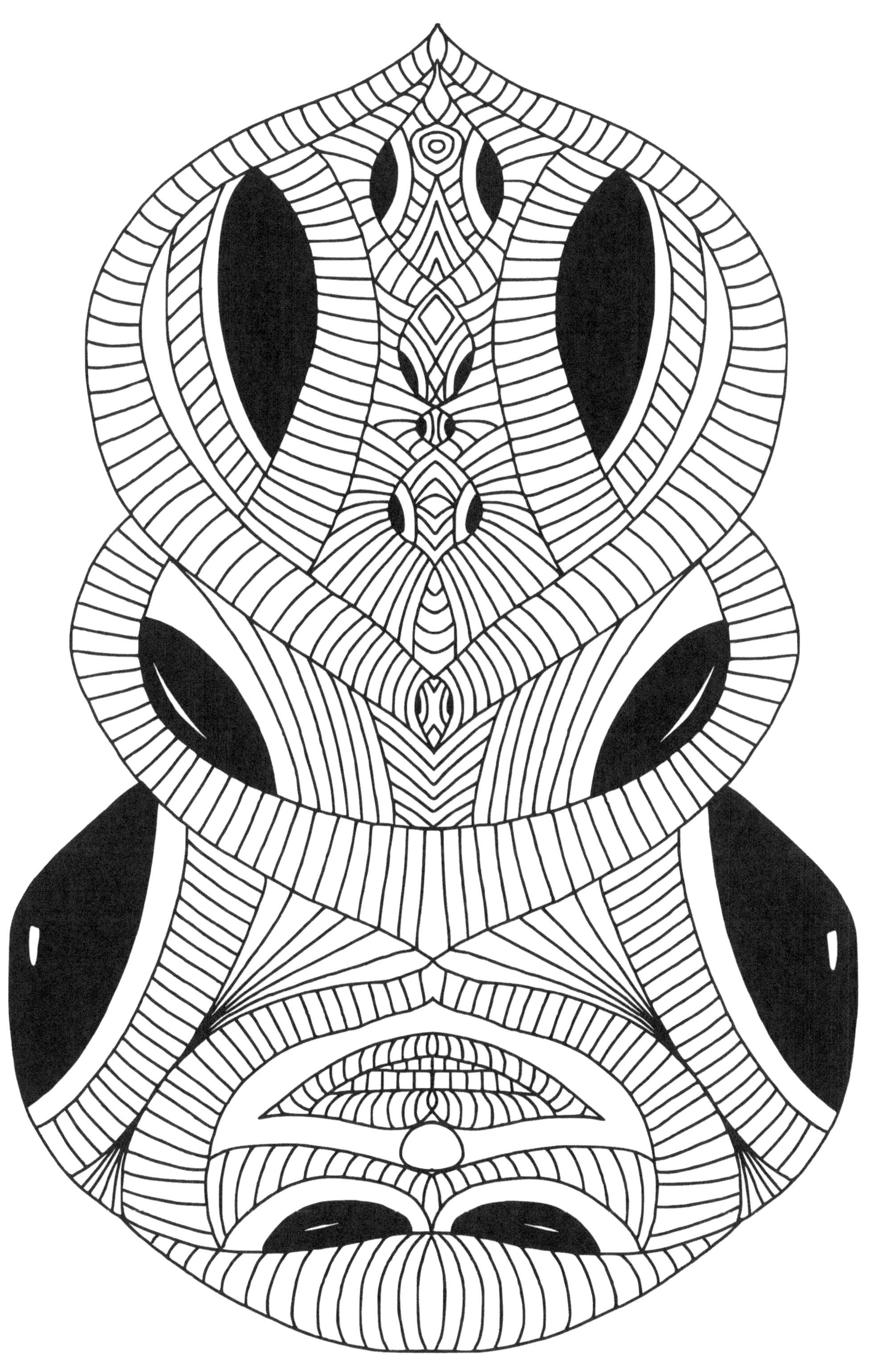

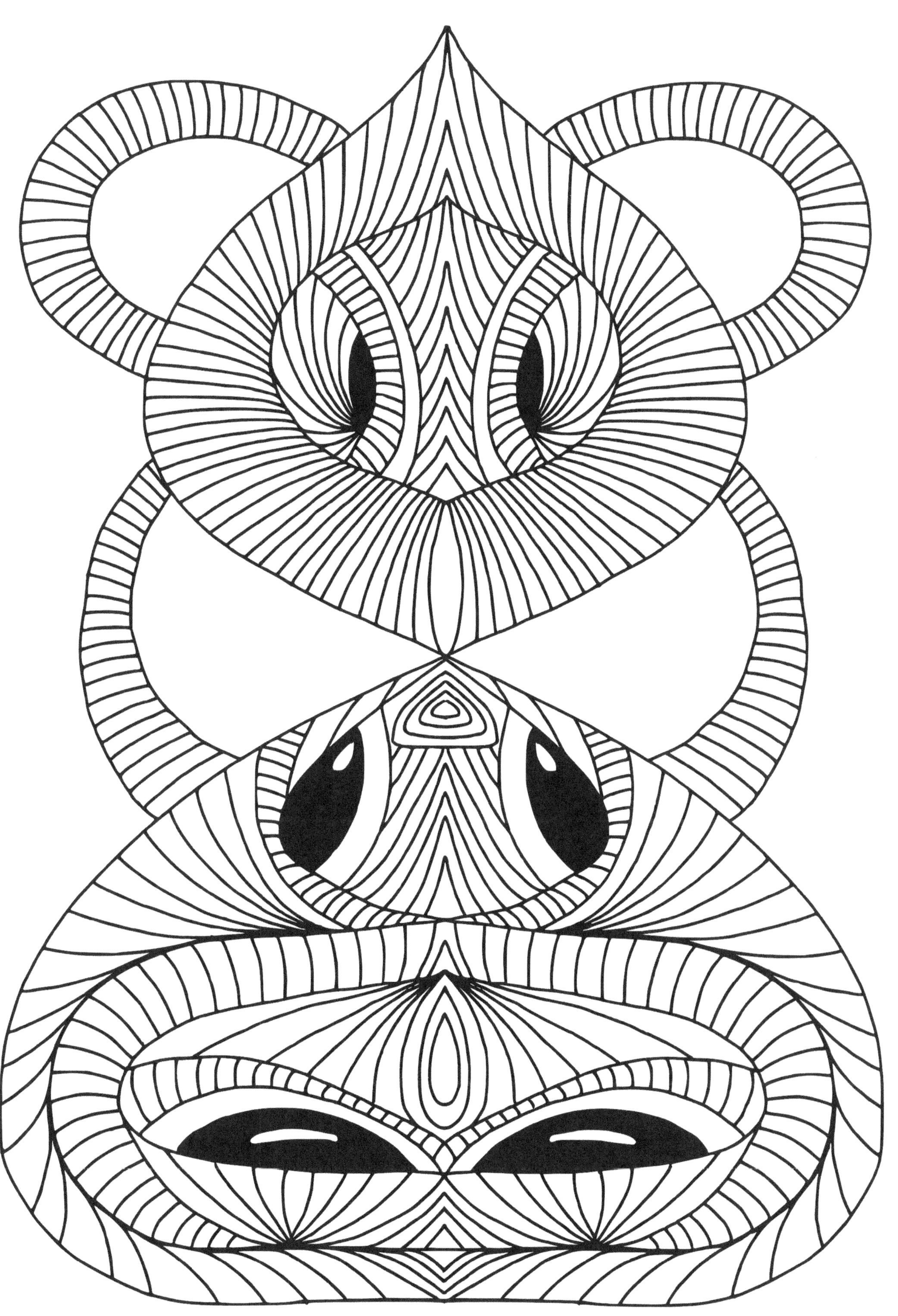

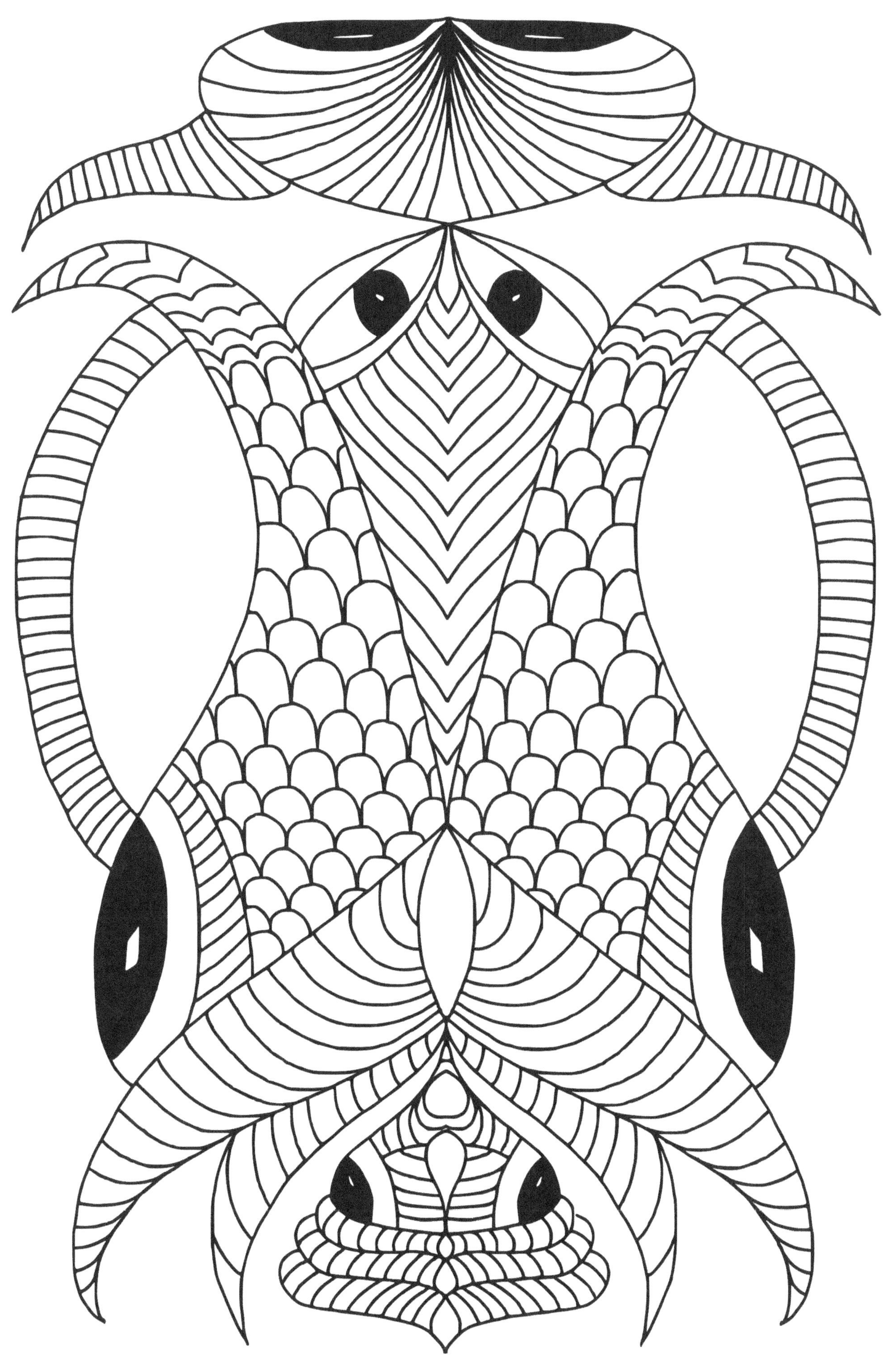

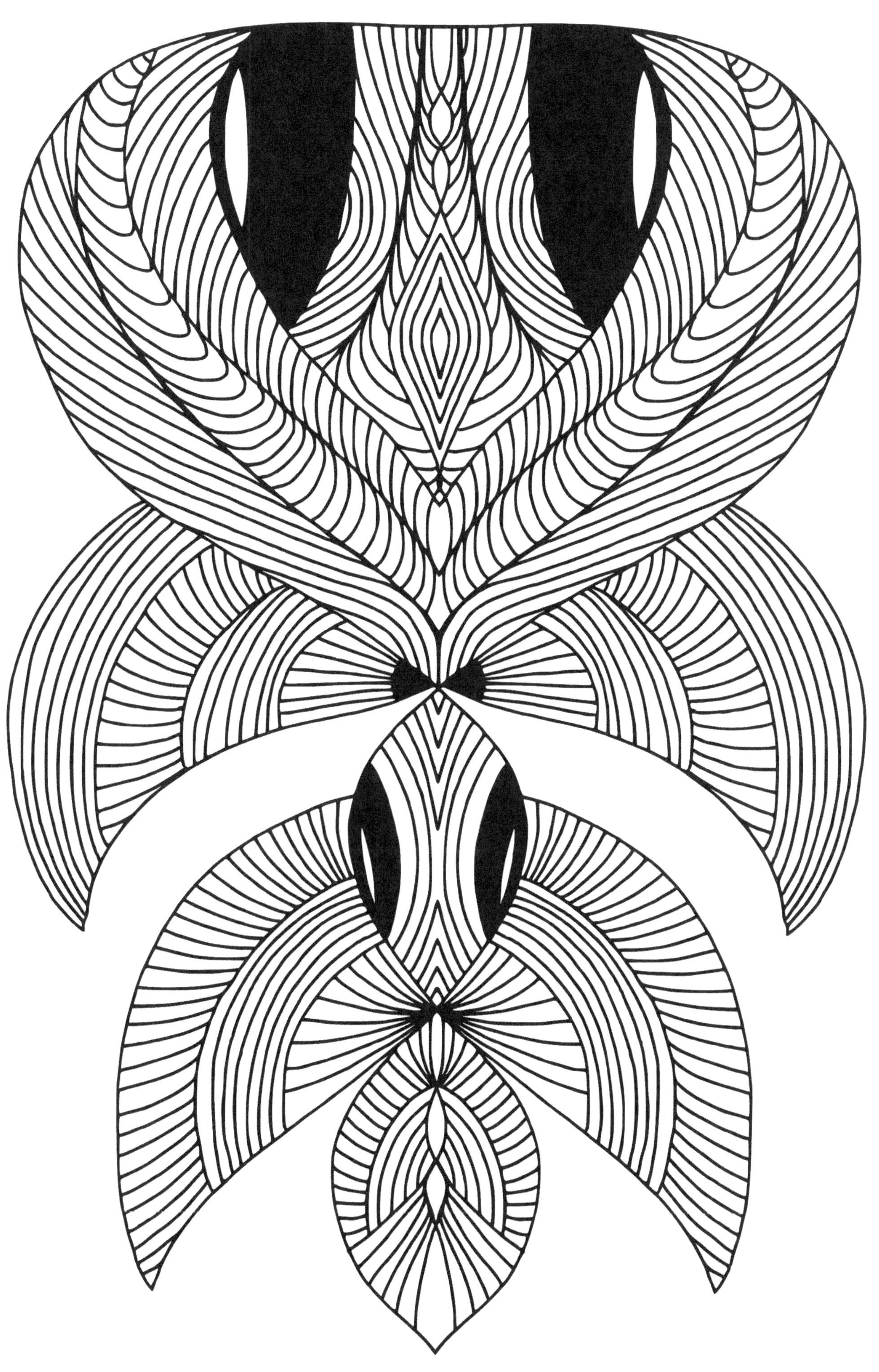

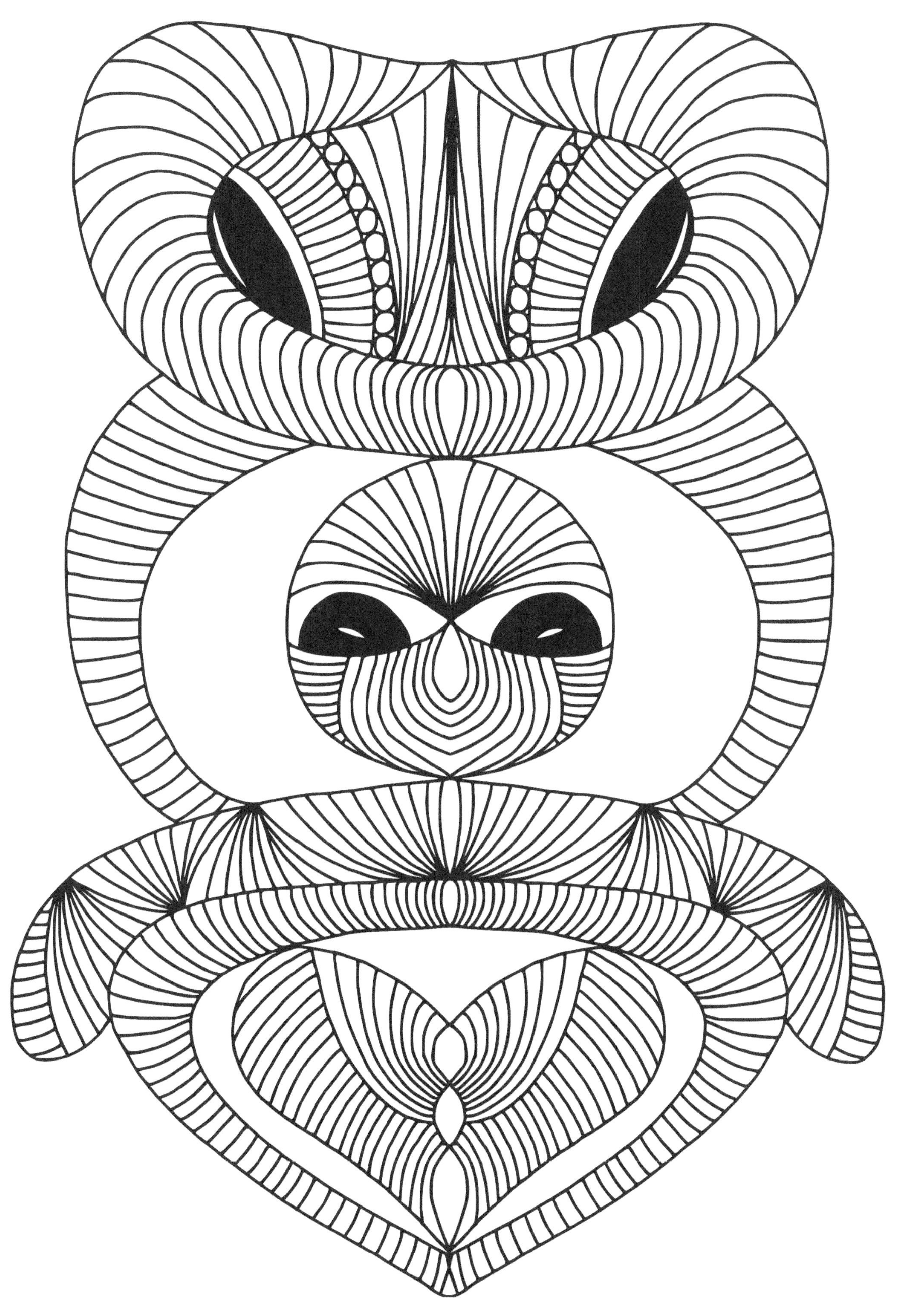

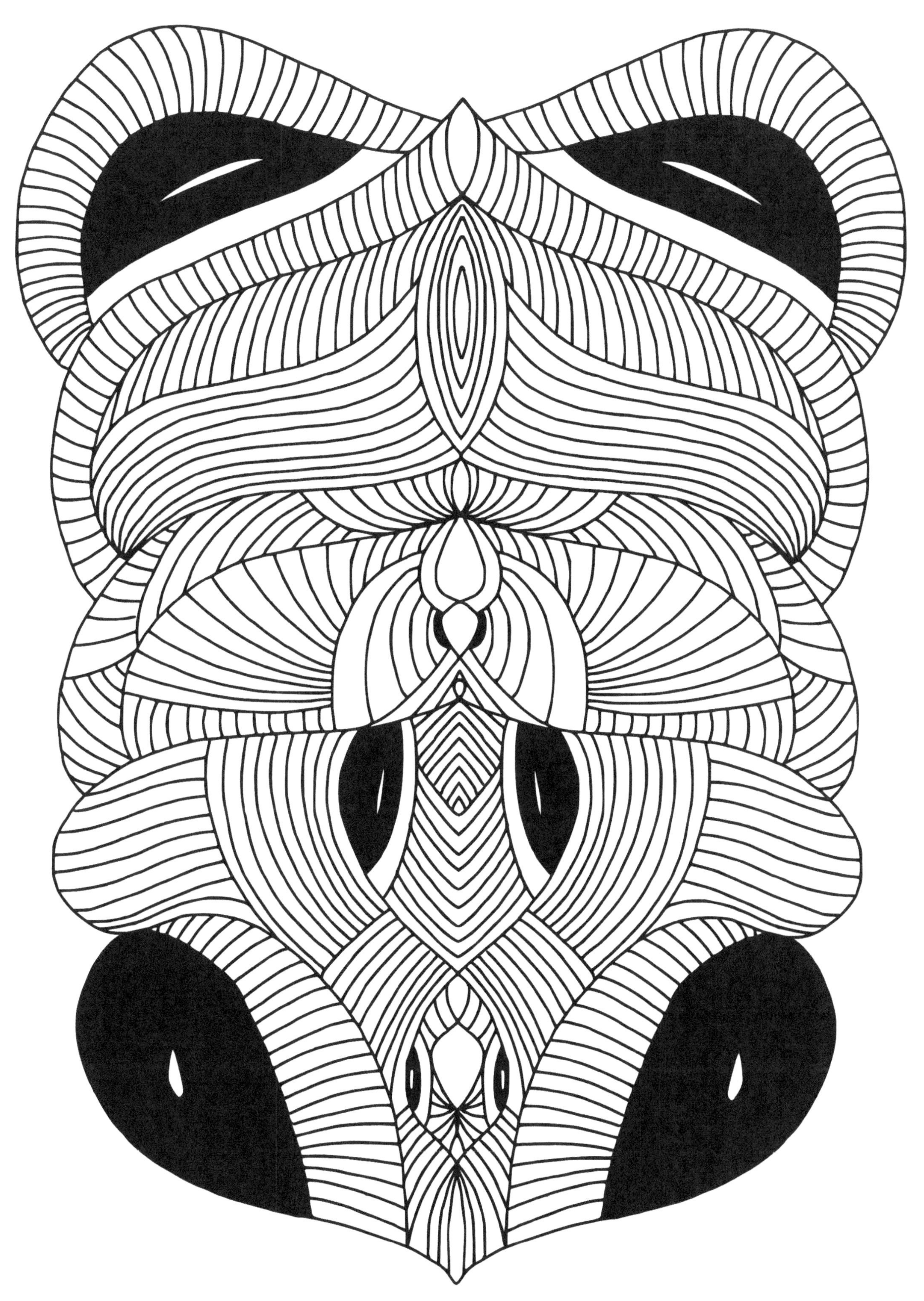

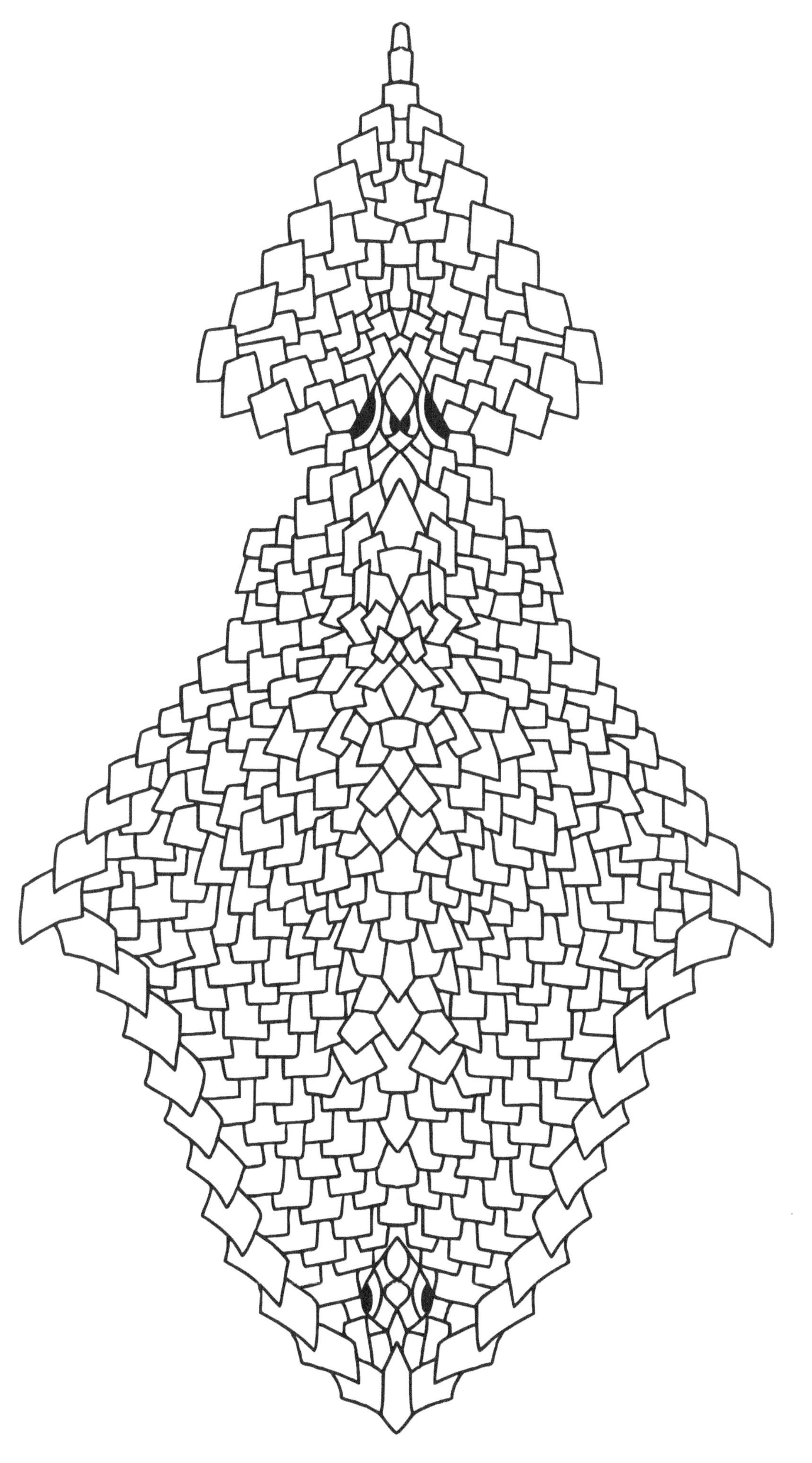

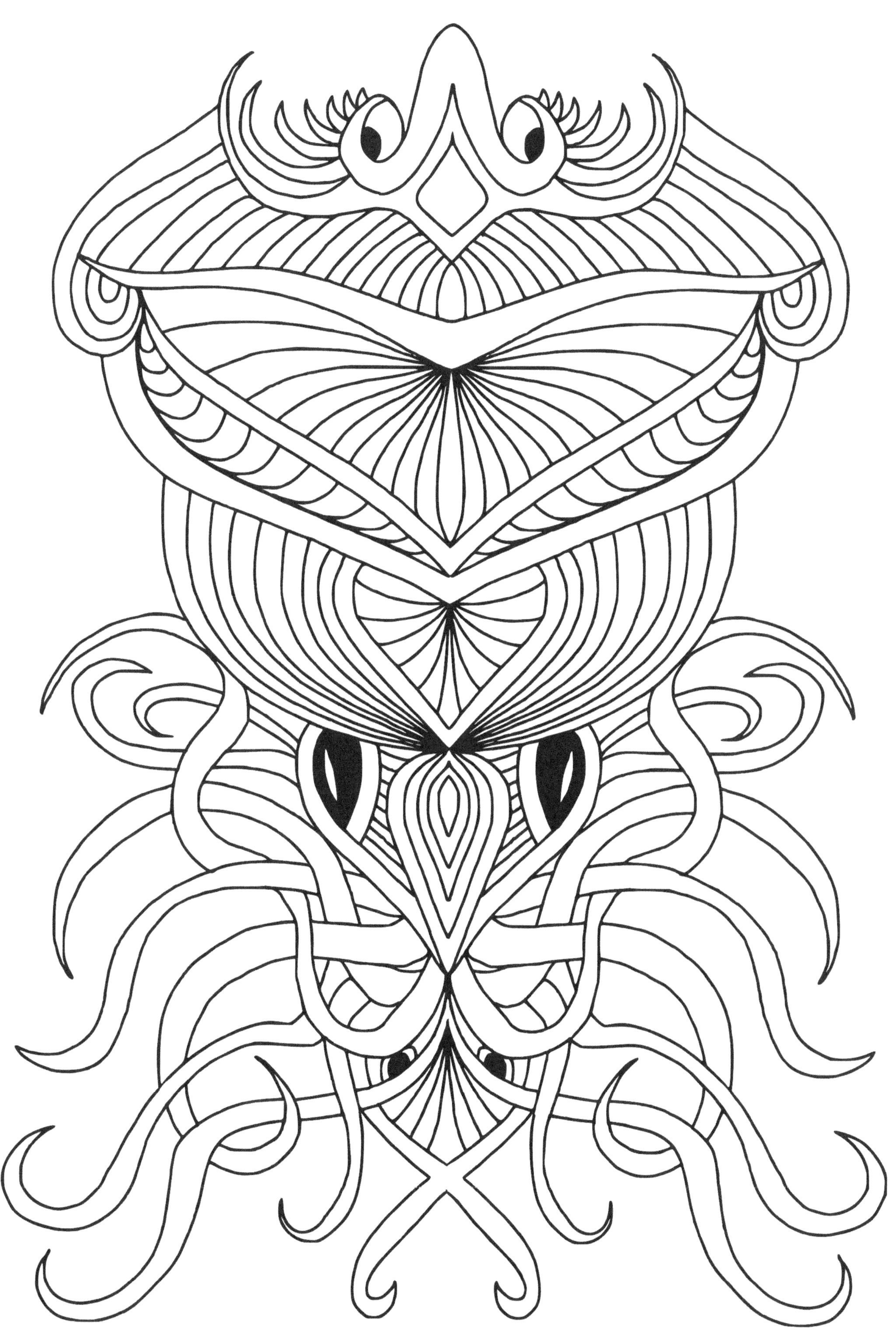

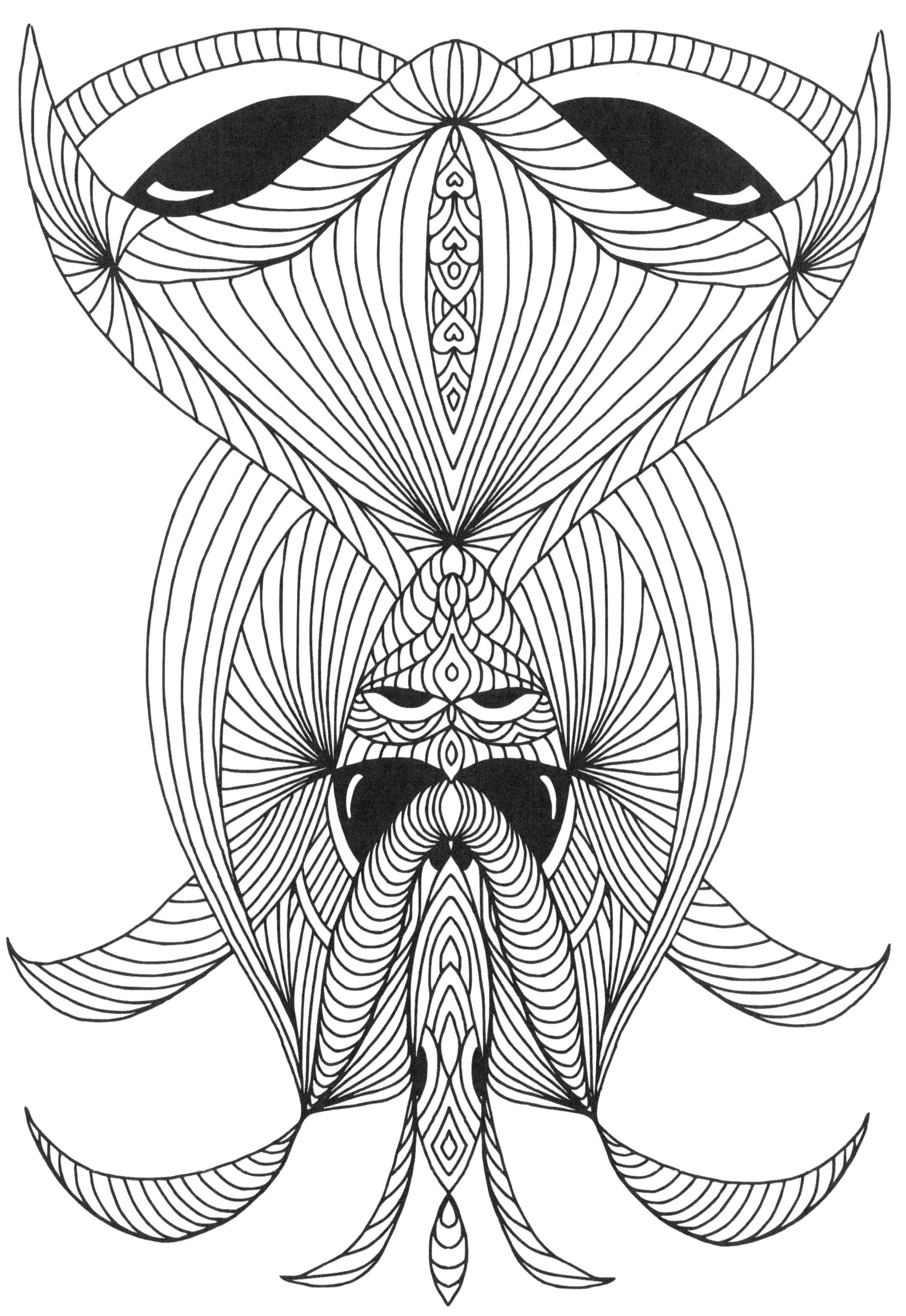

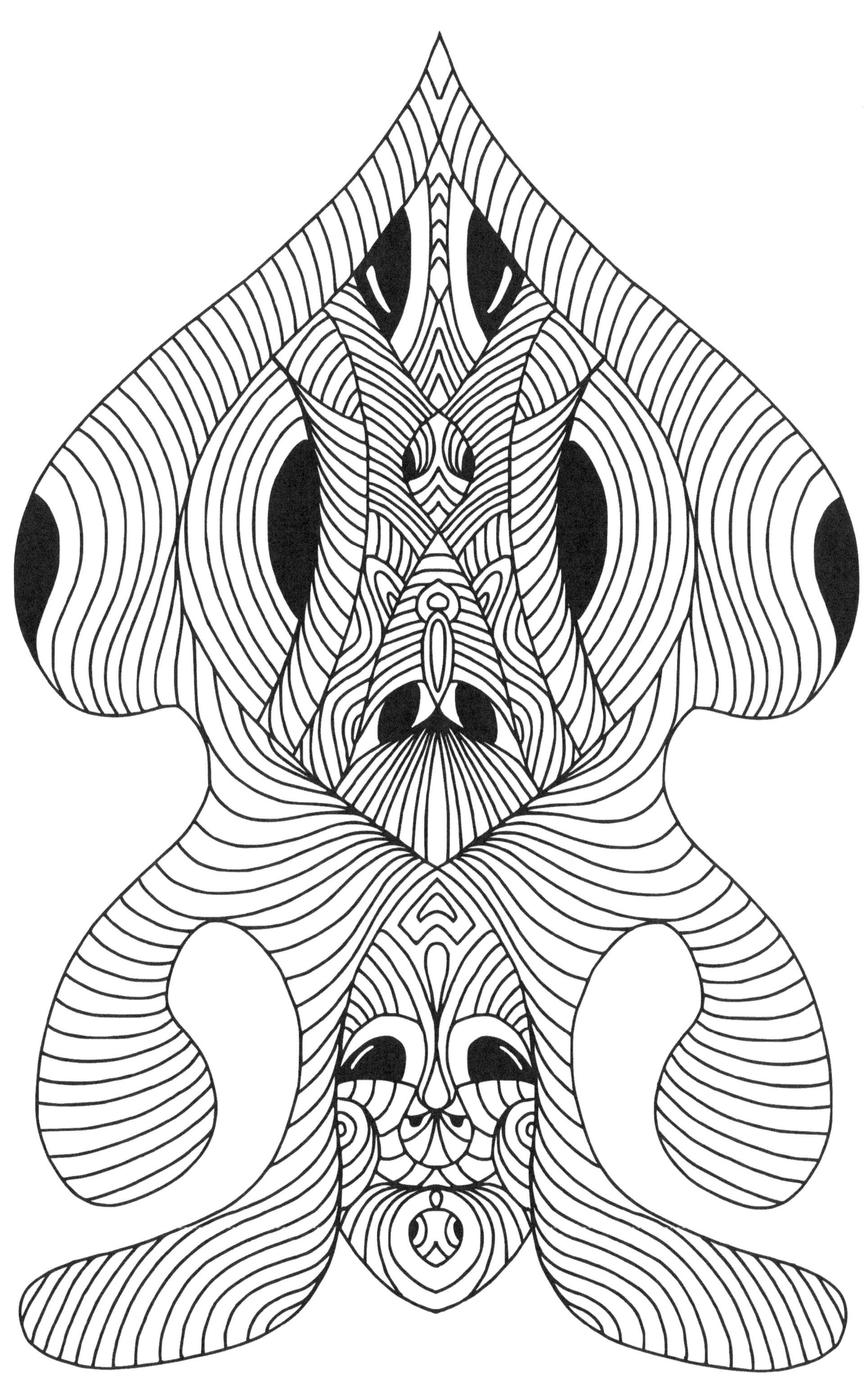

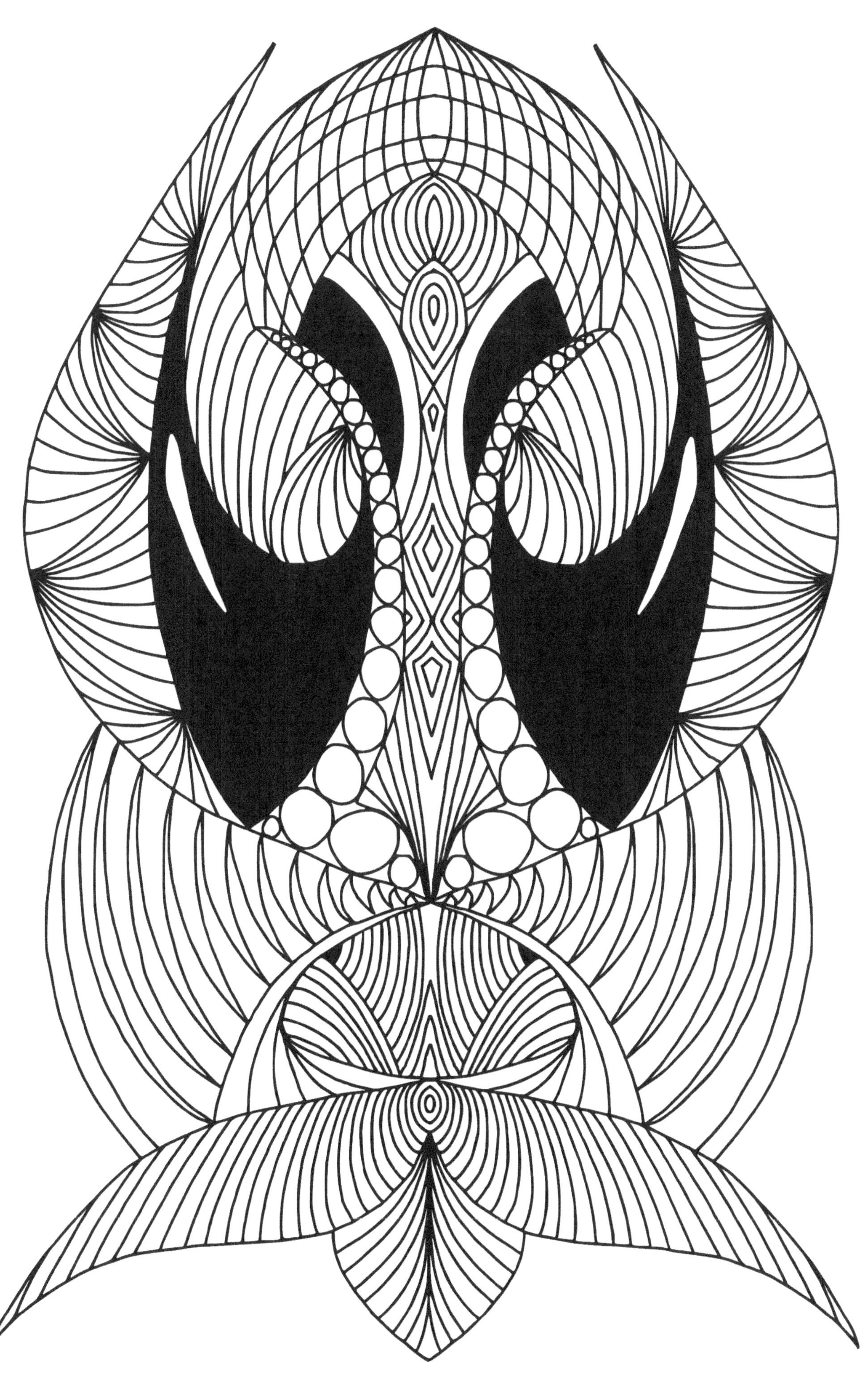

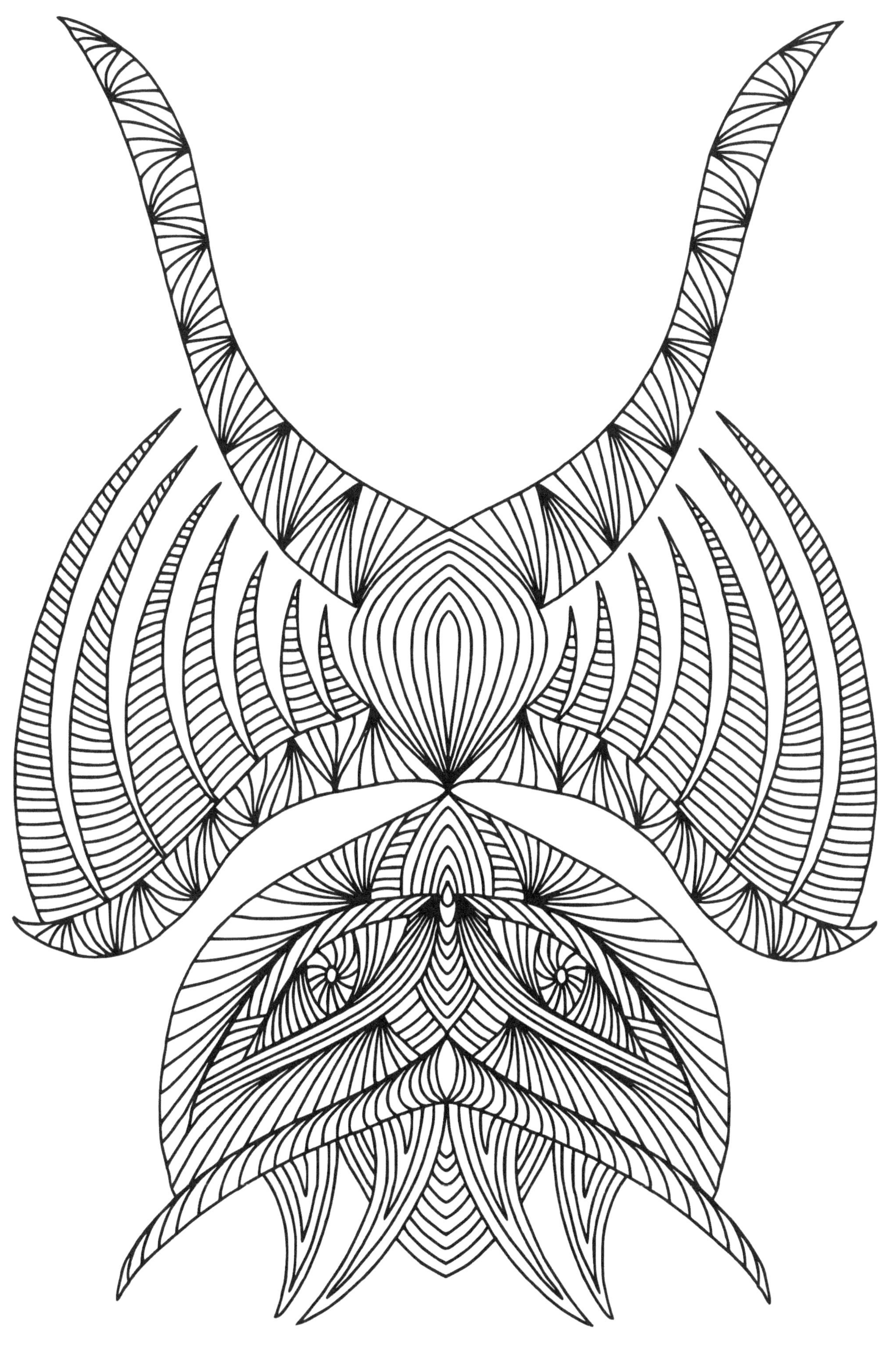

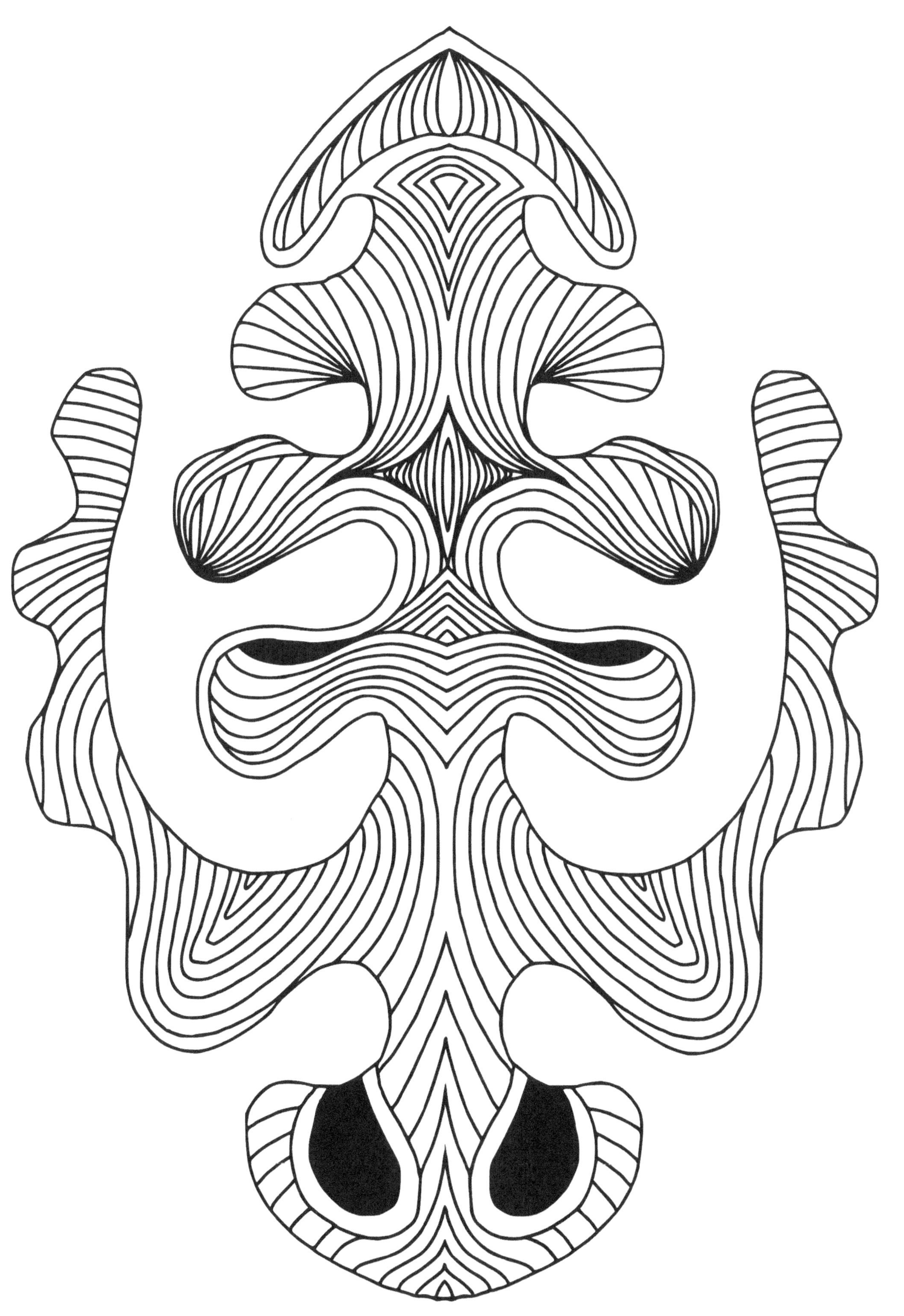

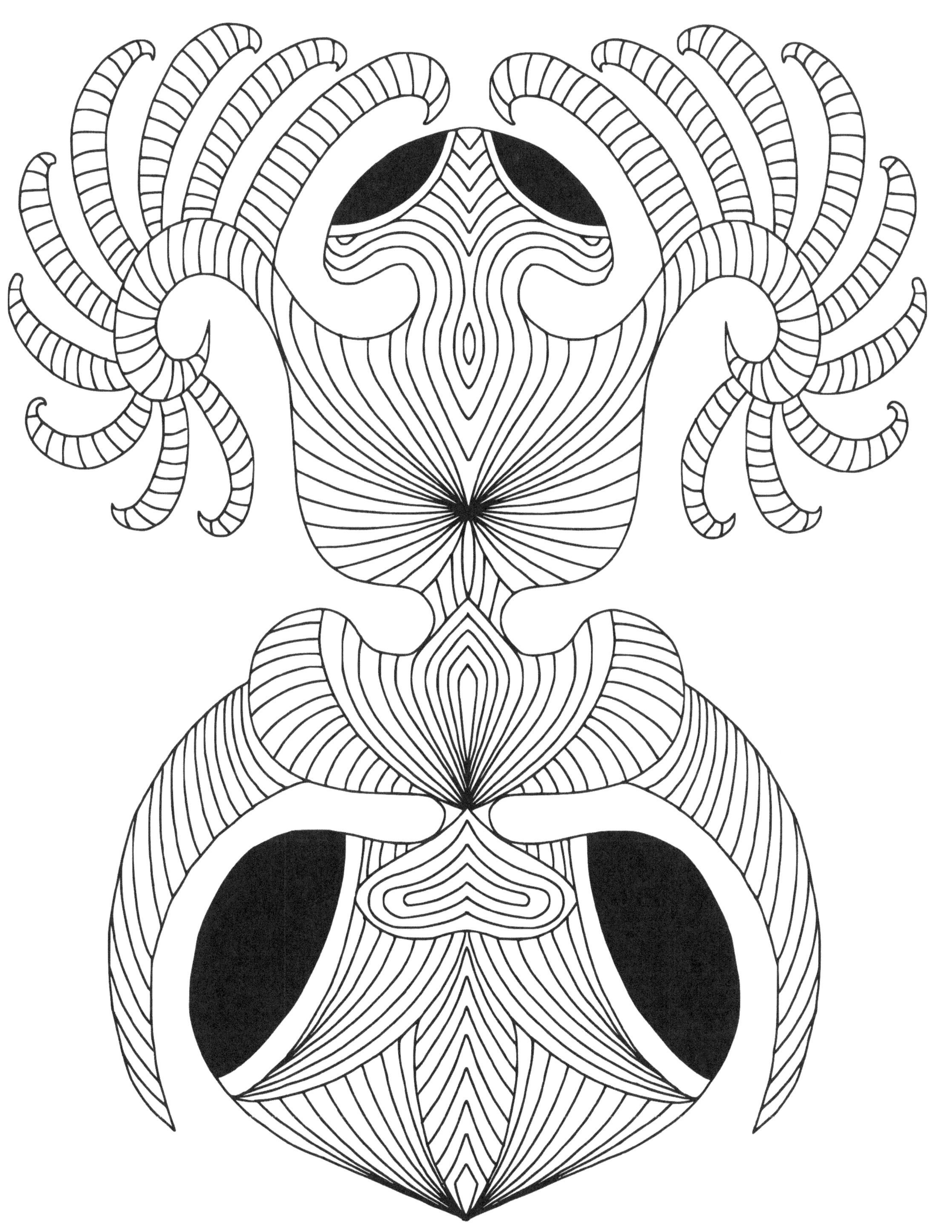

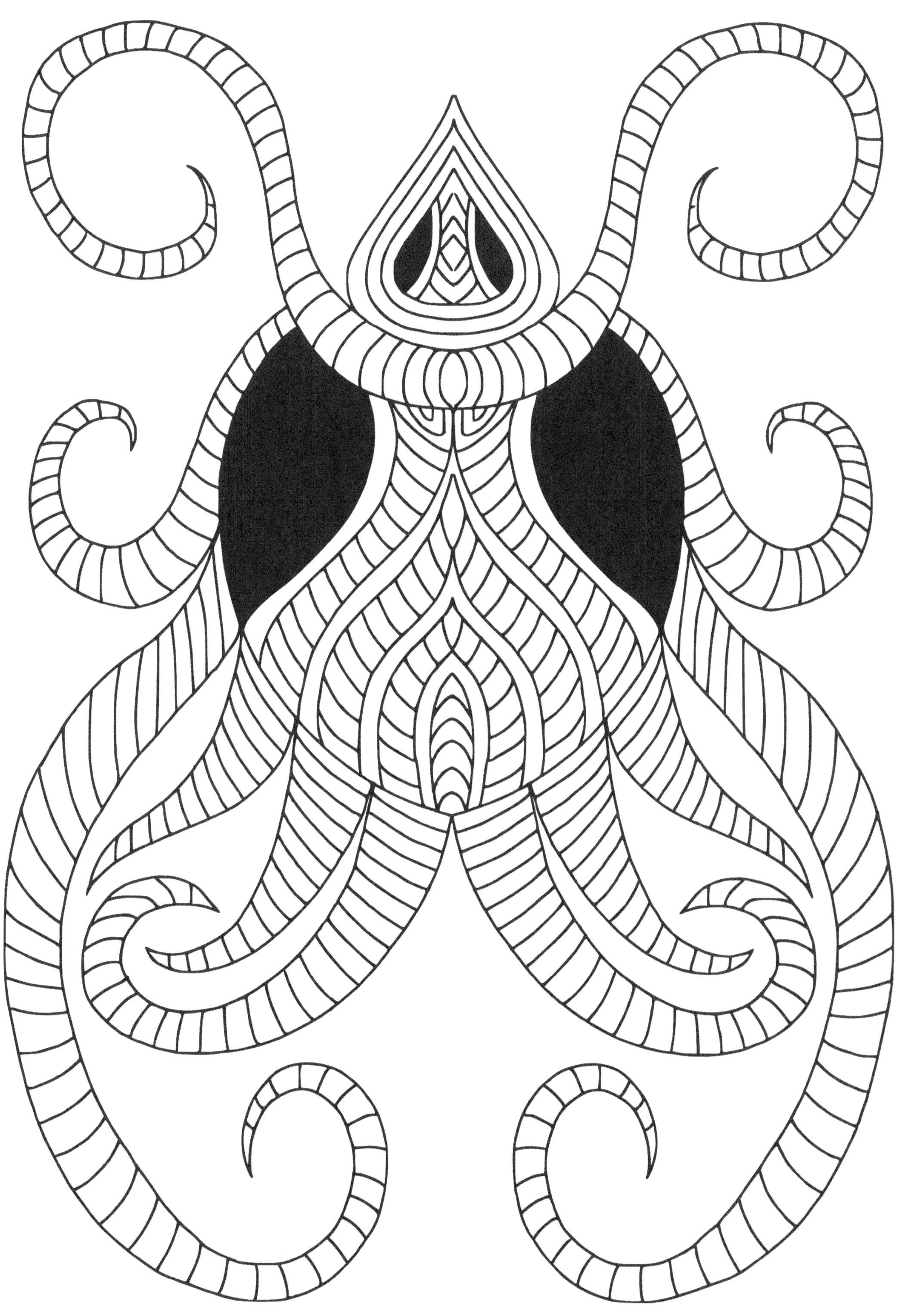

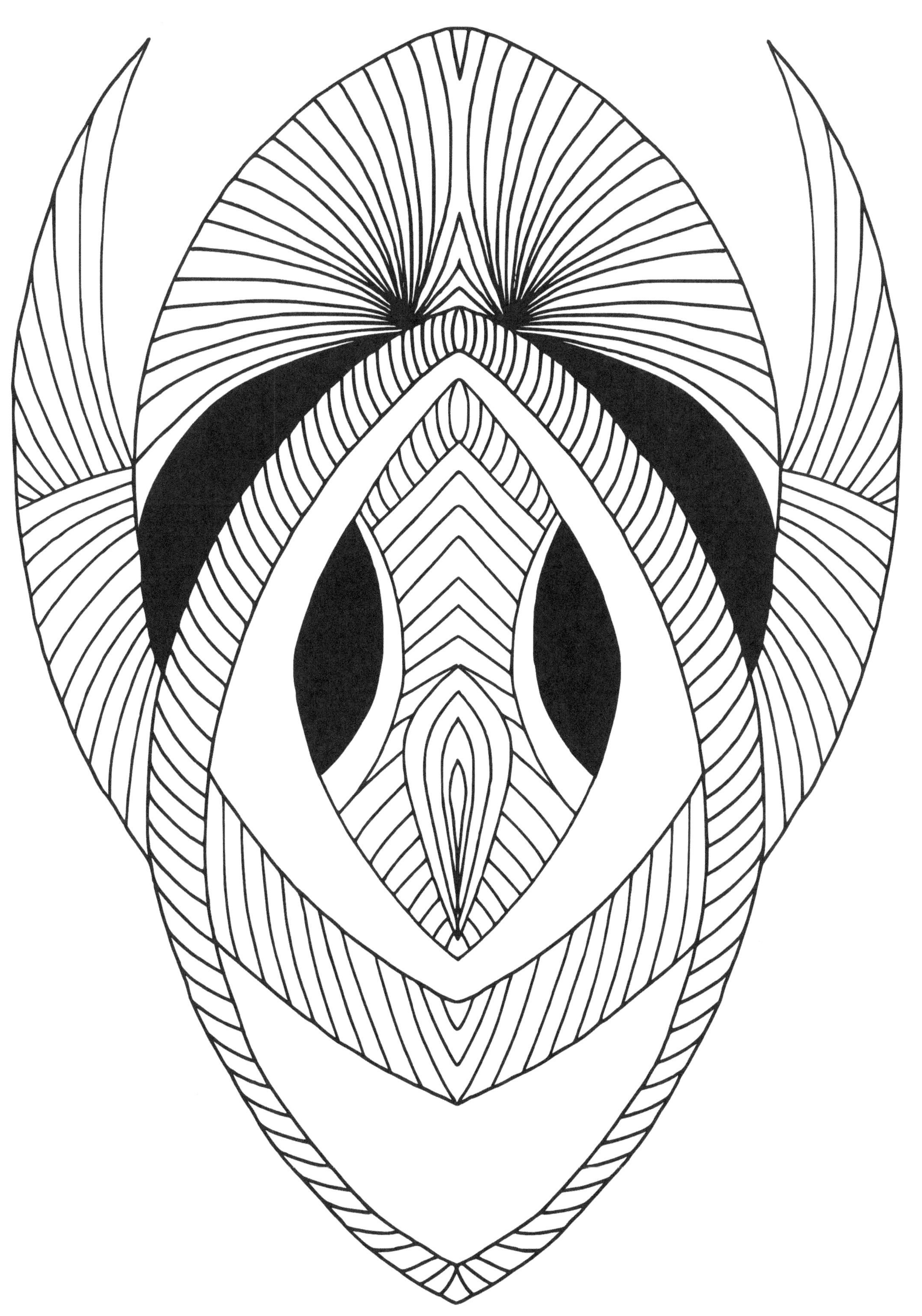

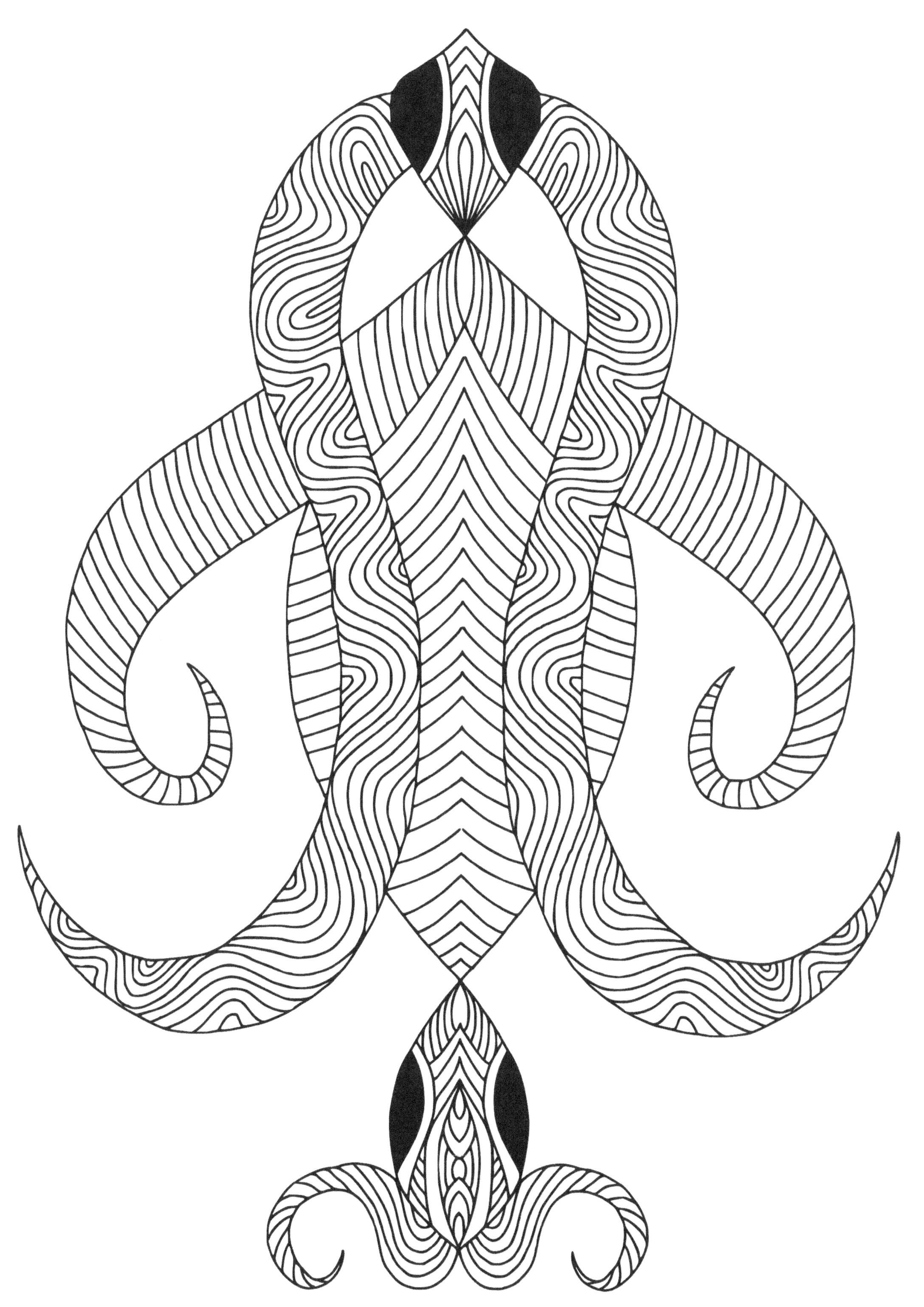

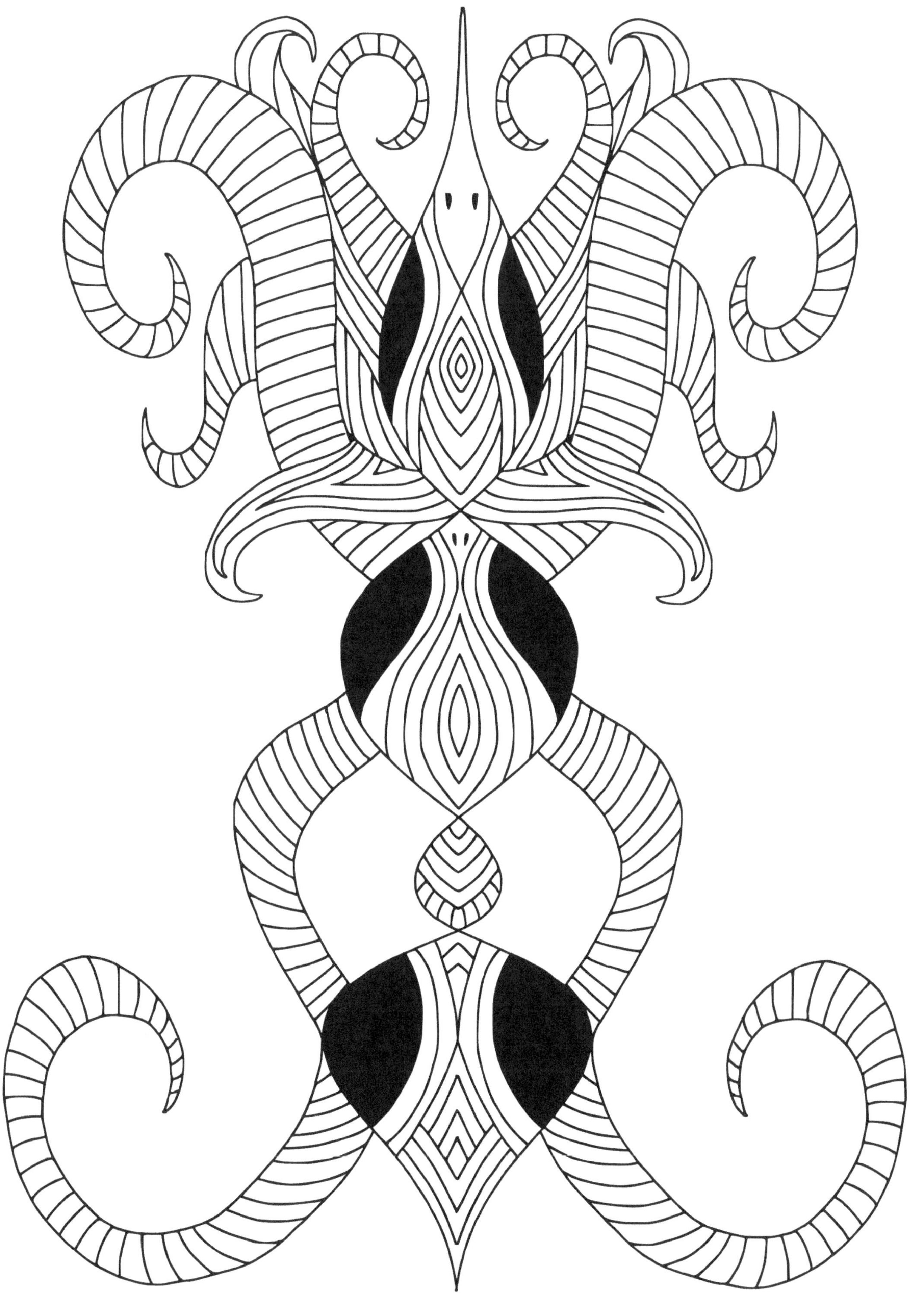

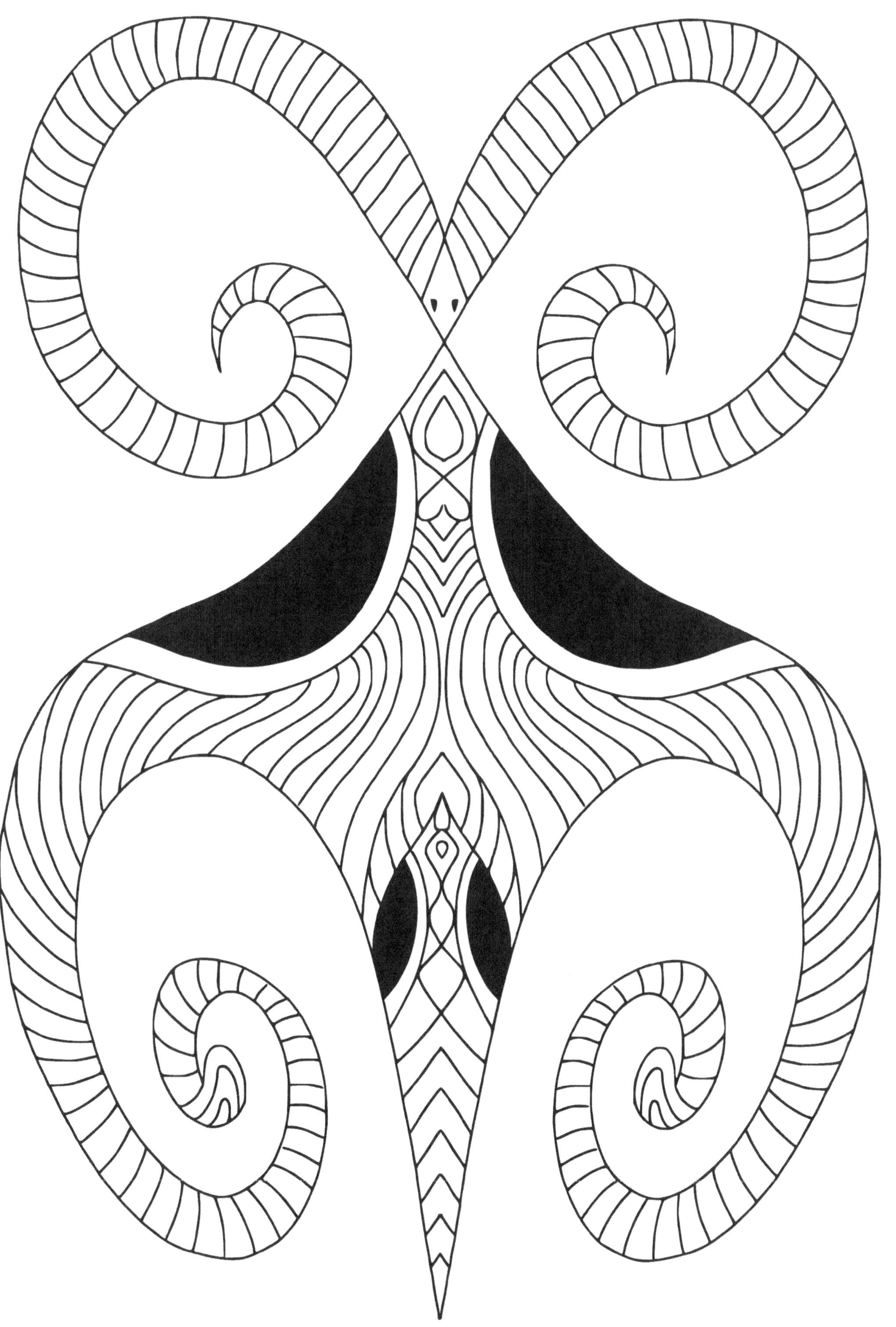

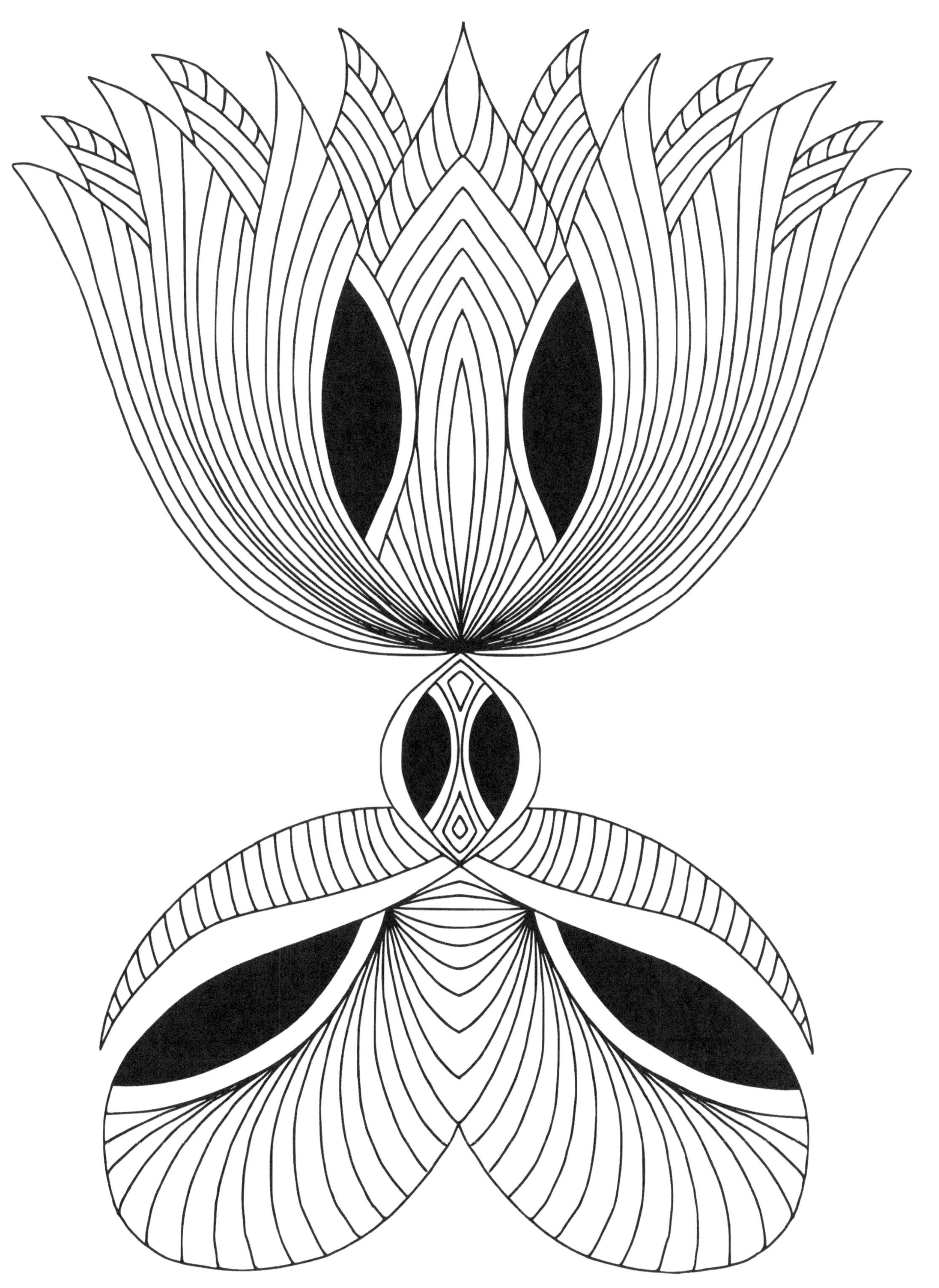

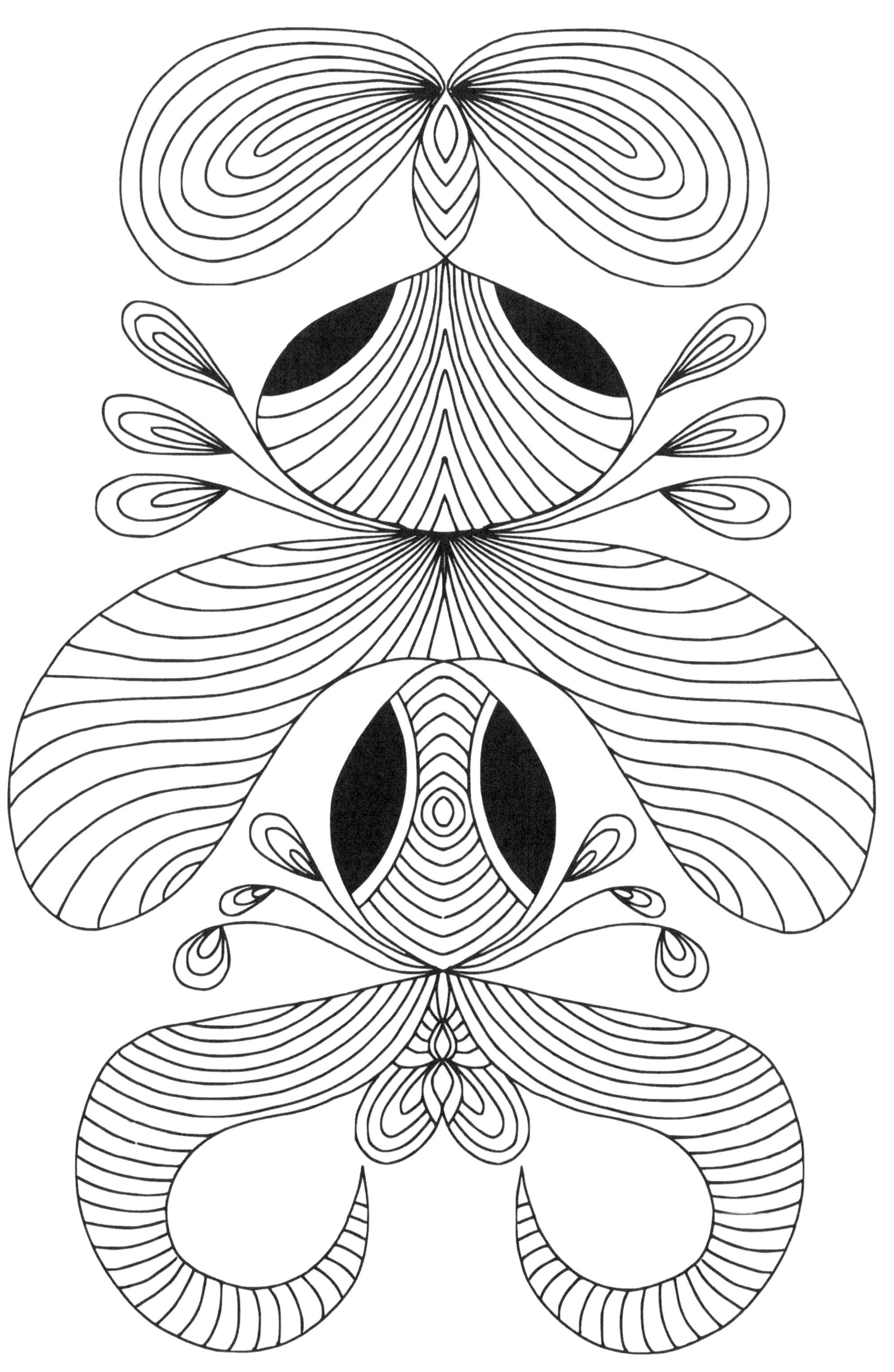

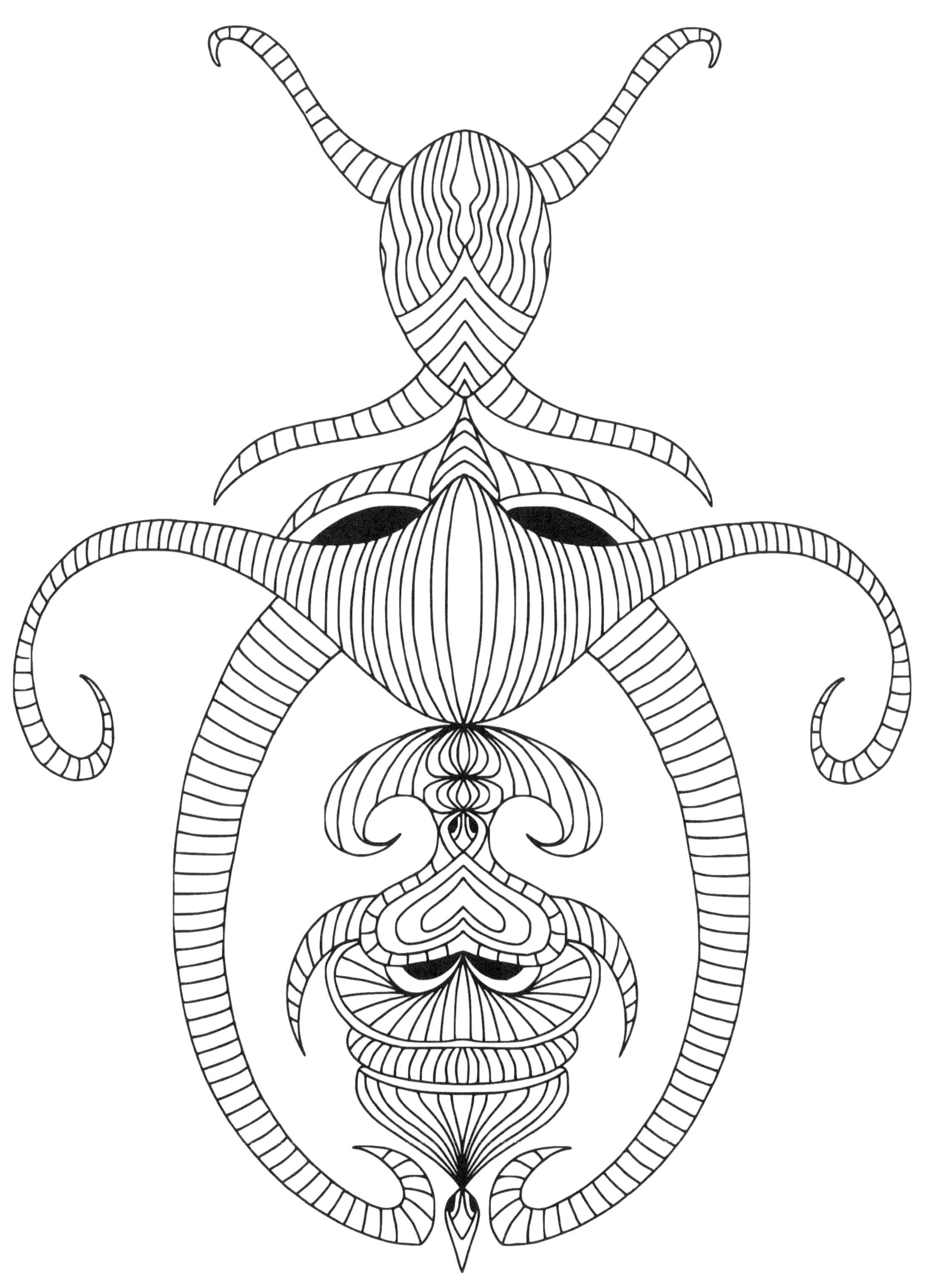

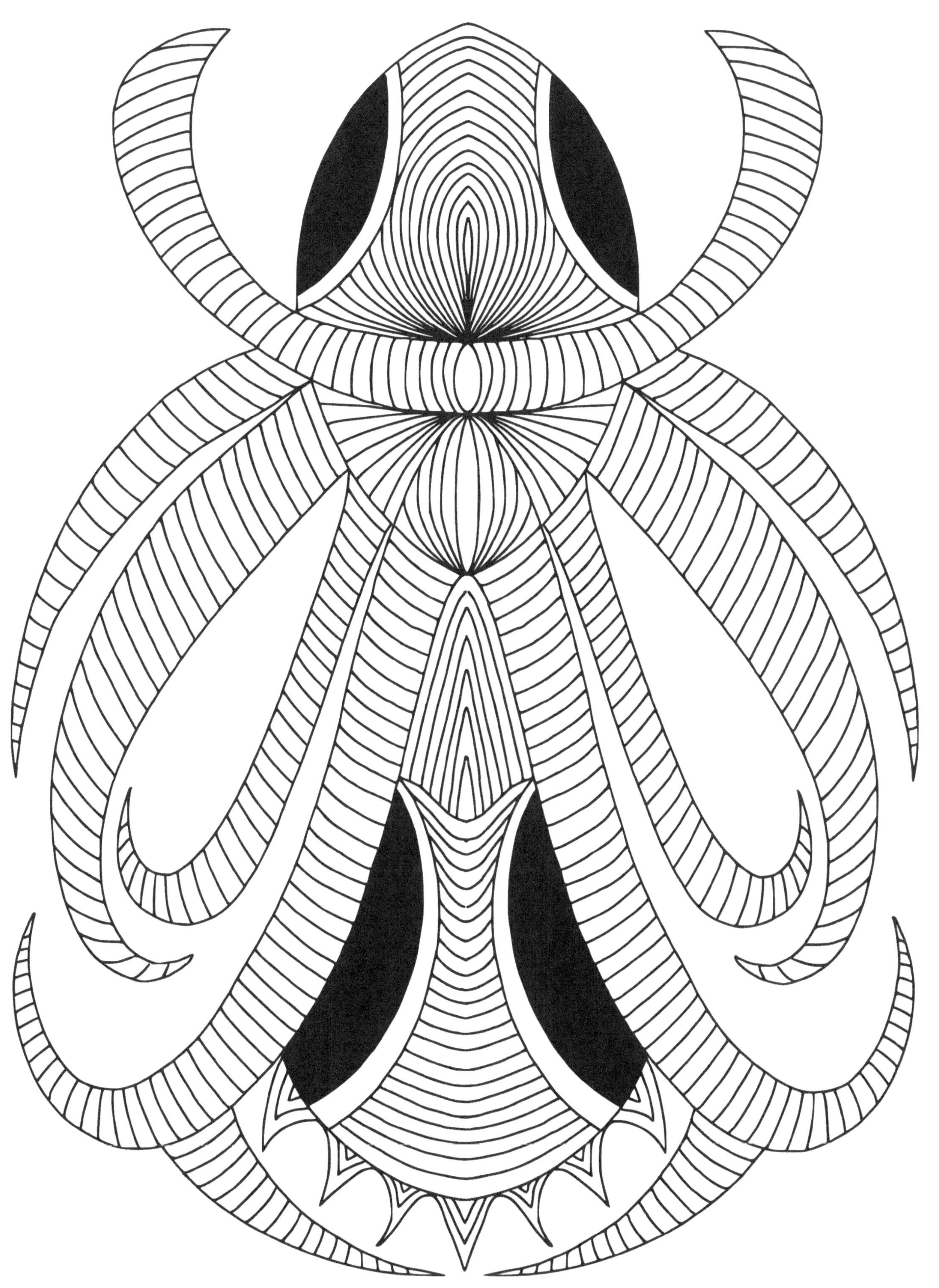

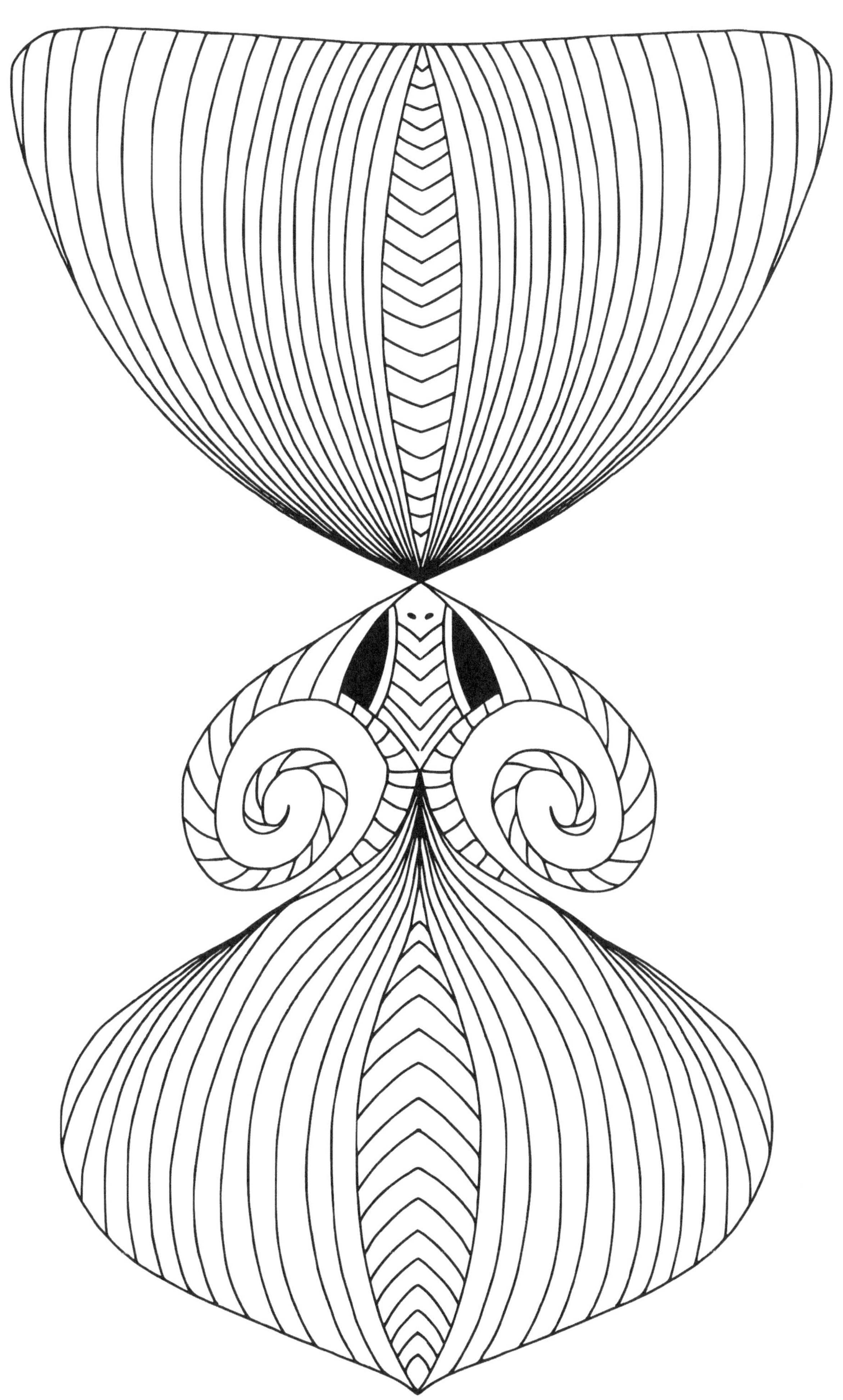

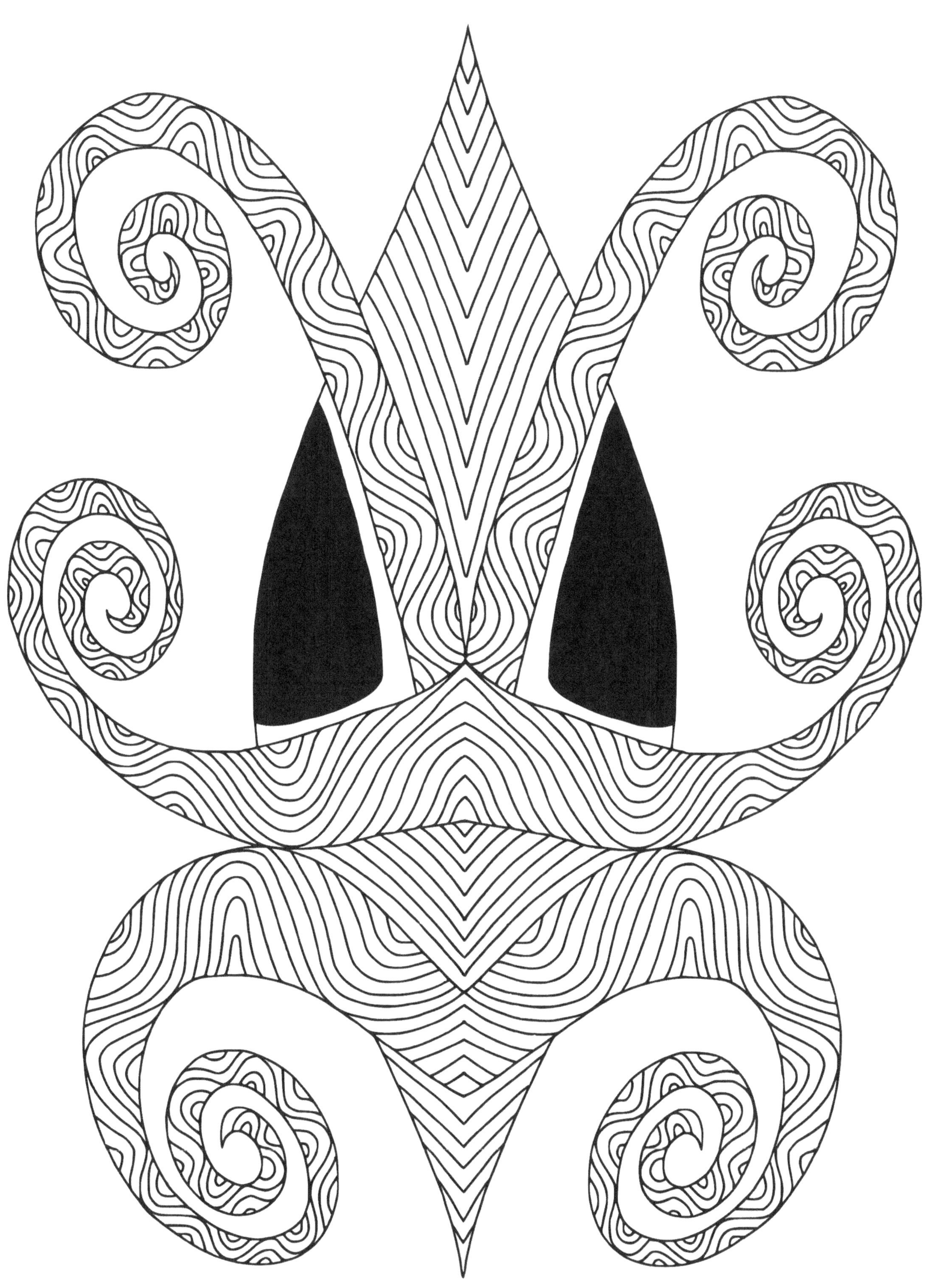

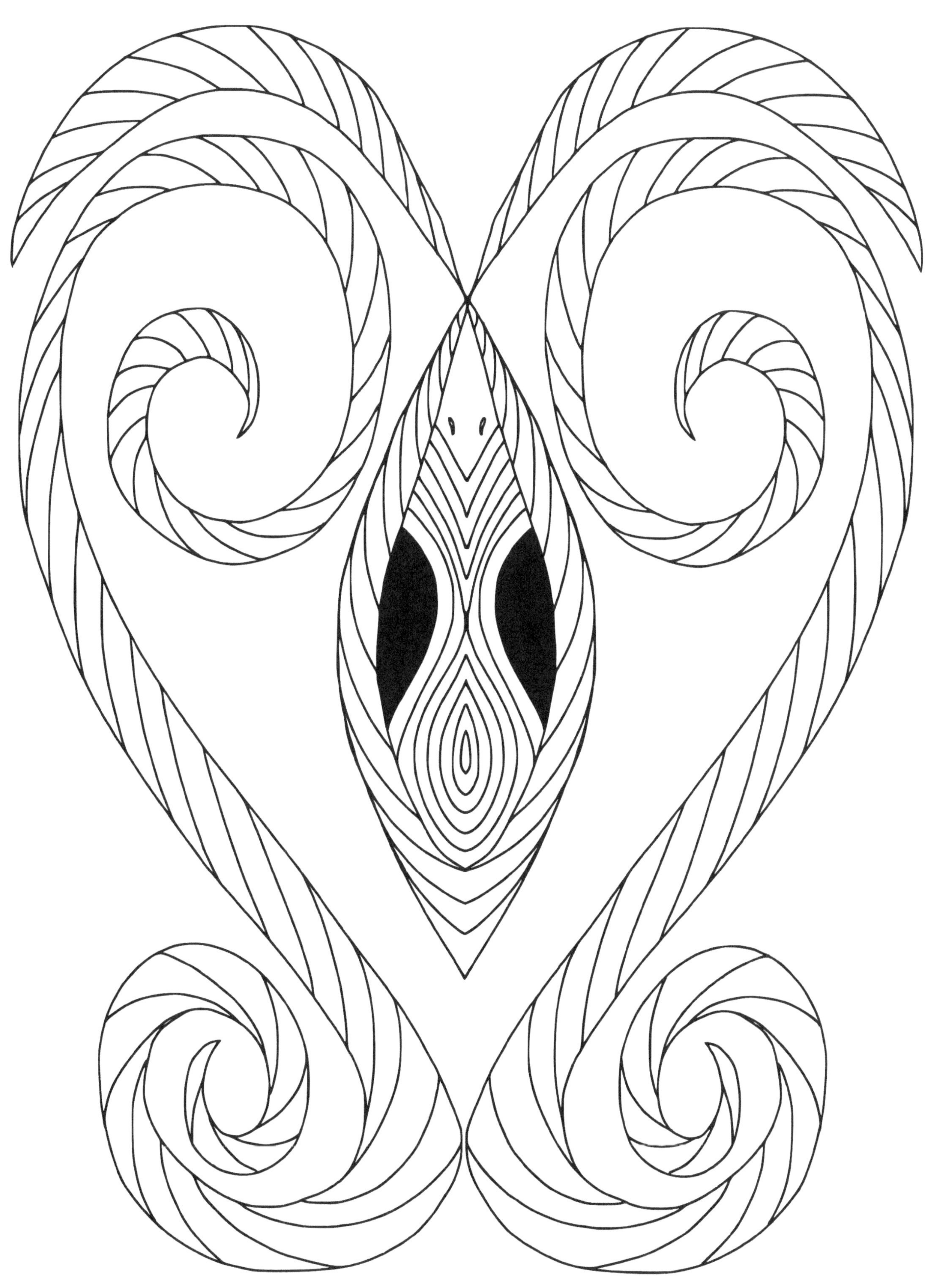

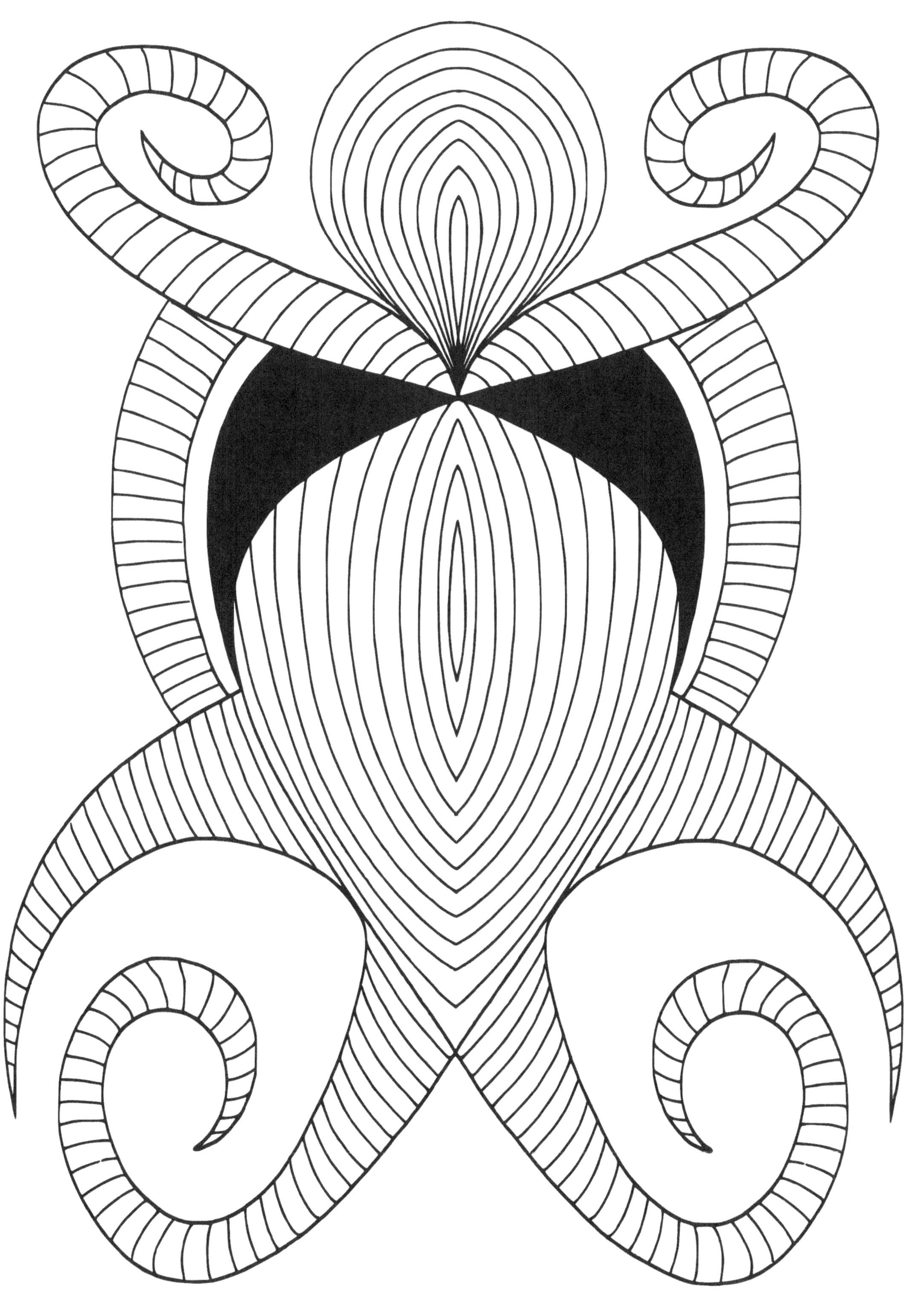

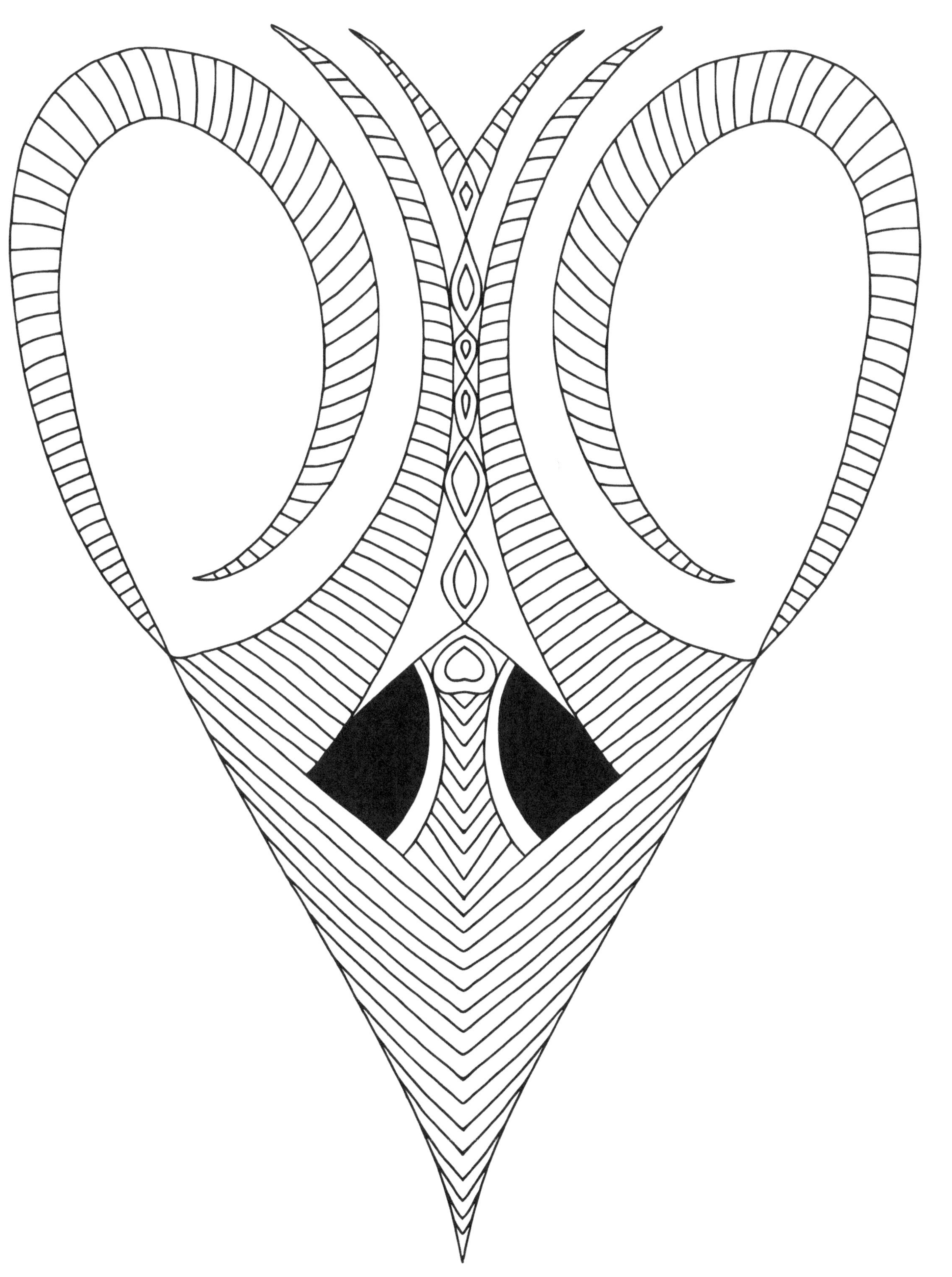

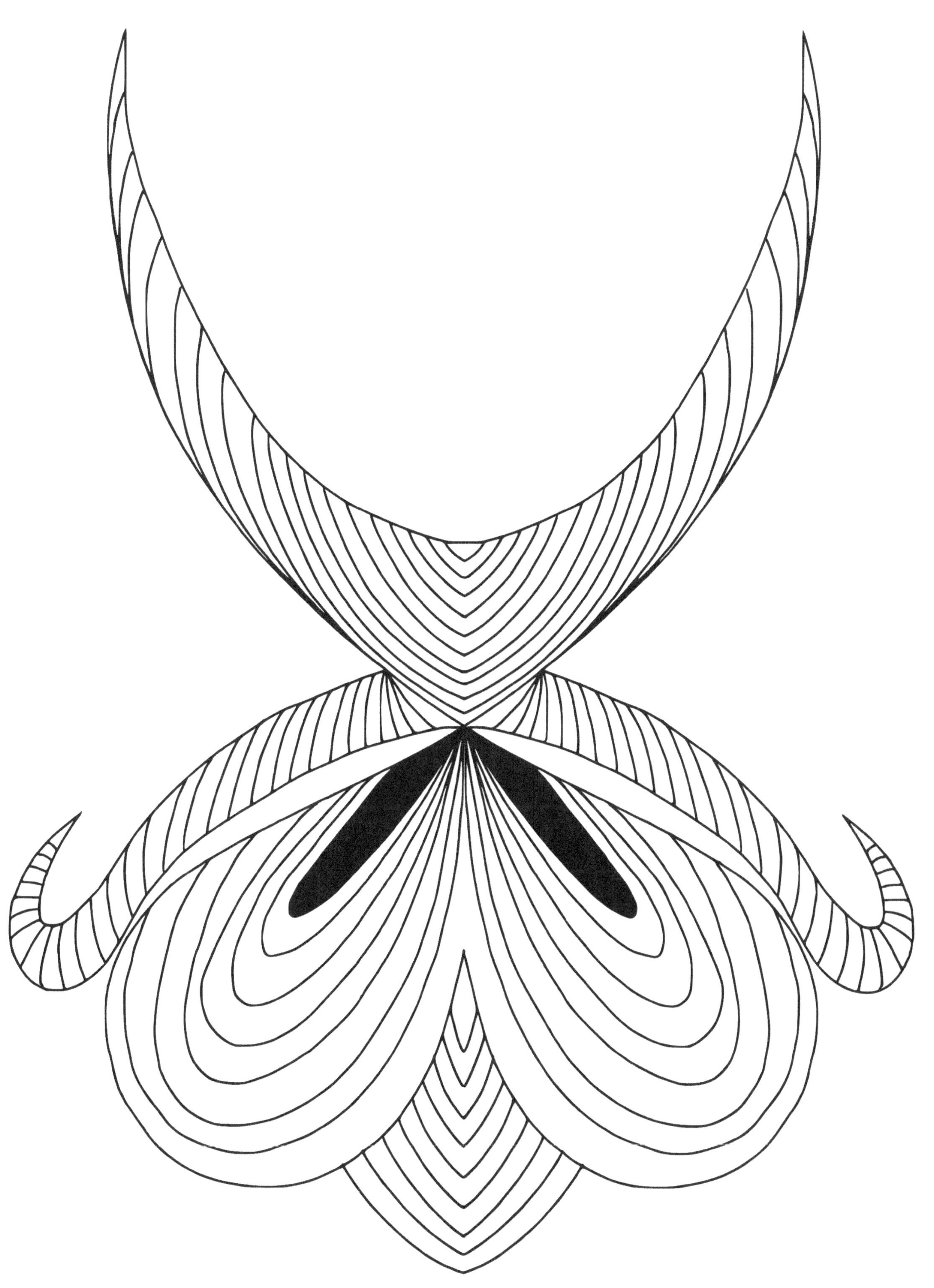

Test your colors here on the samples from
"My Pocket Coloring Companion"
&
"My Coloring Companion"

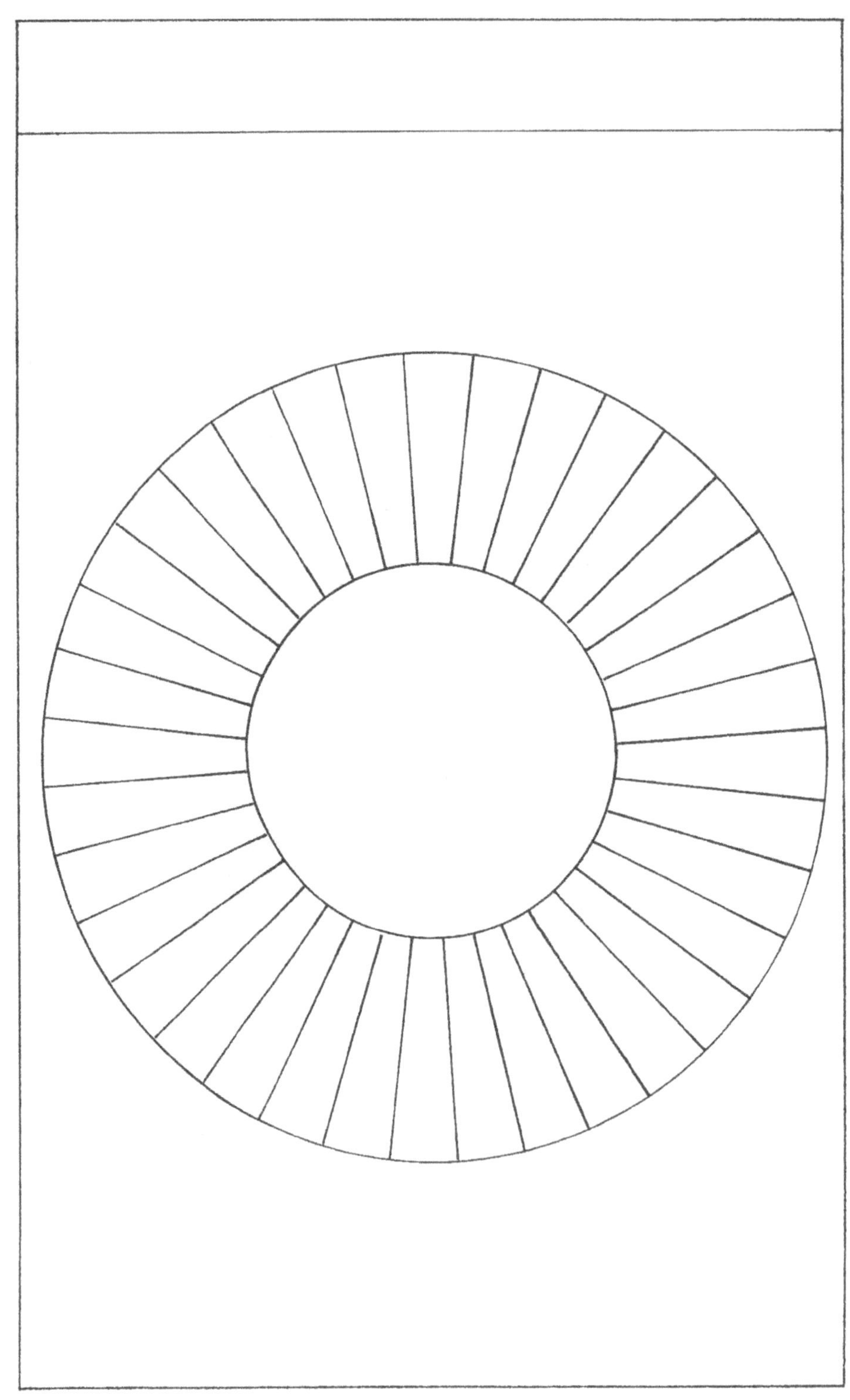

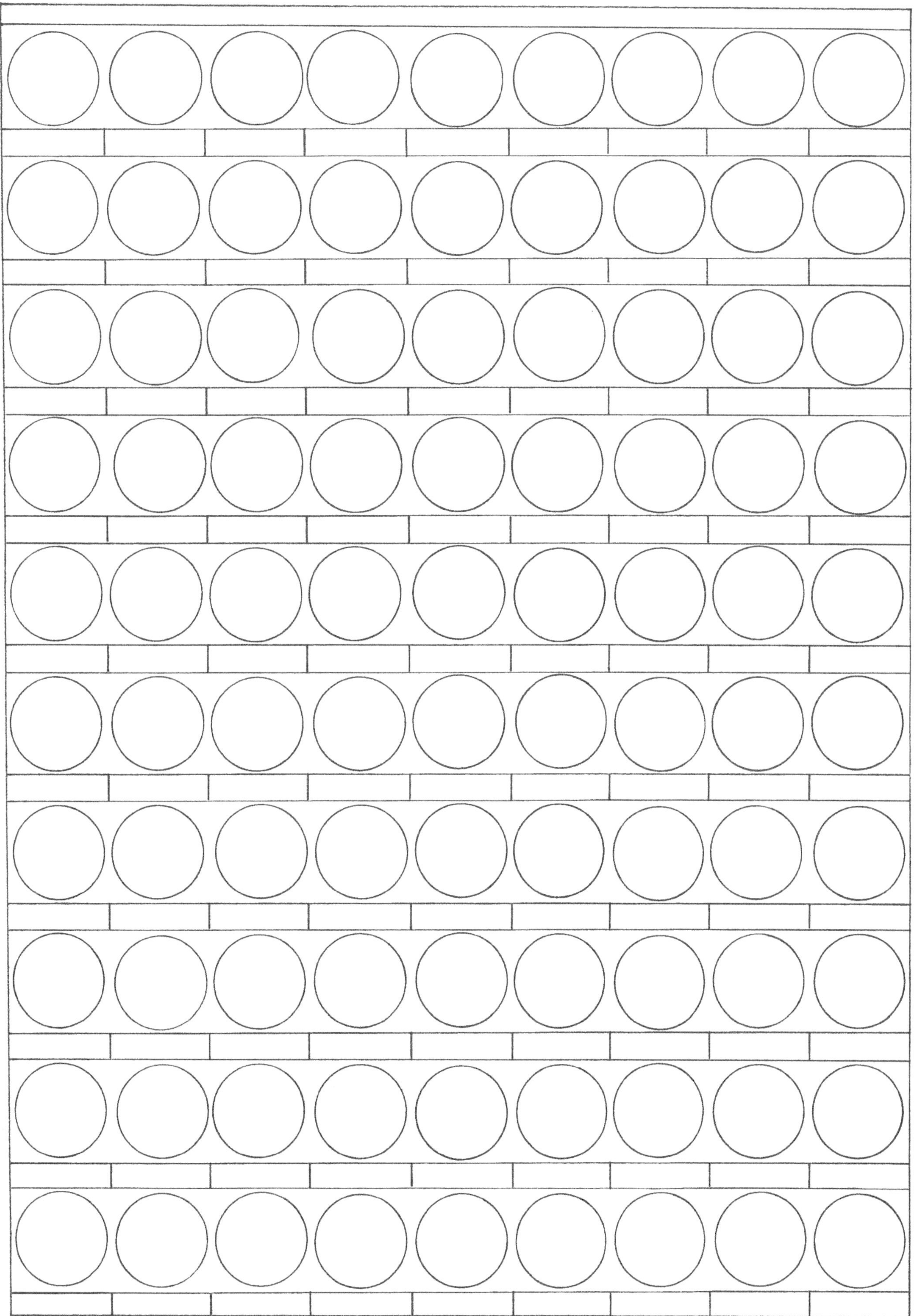

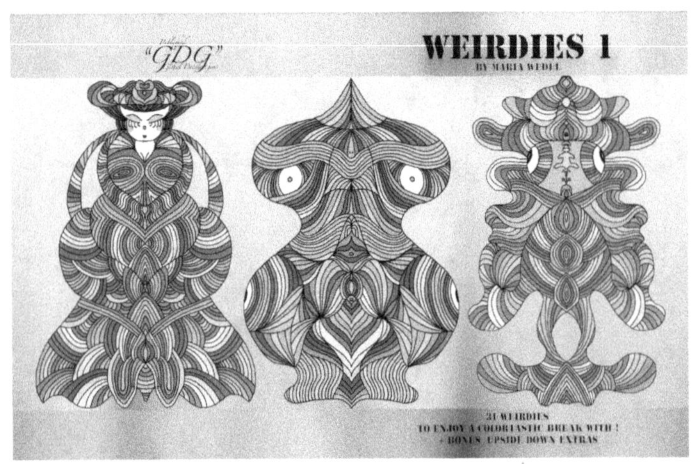
"GDG"
WEIRDIES 1
BY MARIA WEDEL
31 WEIRDIES
TO ENJOY A COLORTASTIC BREAK WITH !
+ BONUS UPSIDE DOWN EXTRAS

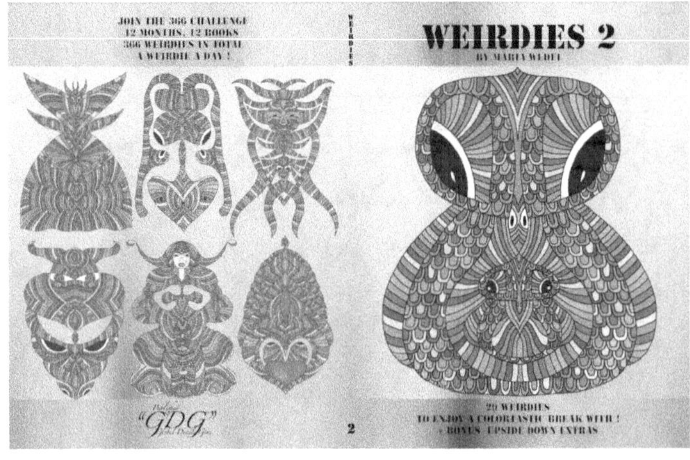
JOIN THE 366 CHALLENGE
12 MONTHS, 12 BOOKS
366 WEIRDIES IN TOTAL
A WEIRDIE A DAY !
WEIRDIES 2
BY MARIA WEDEL
"GDG"
2
29 WEIRDIES
TO ENJOY A COLORTASTIC BREAK WITH !
+ BONUS UPSIDE DOWN EXTRAS

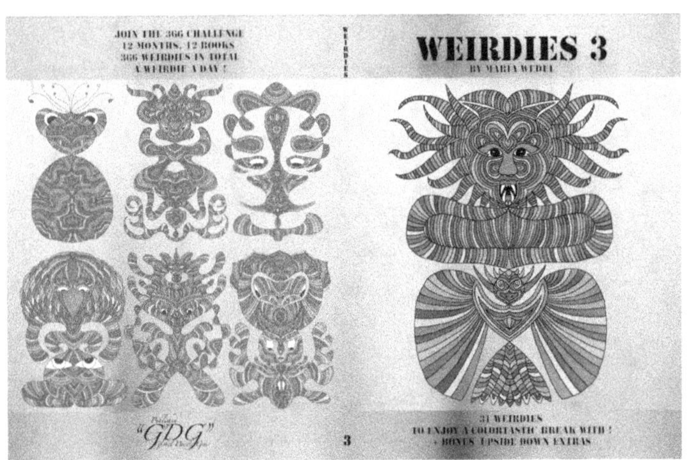
JOIN THE 366 CHALLENGE
12 MONTHS, 12 BOOKS
366 WEIRDIES IN TOTAL
A WEIRDIE A DAY !
WEIRDIES 3
BY MARIA WEDEL
"GDG"
3
31 WEIRDIES
TO ENJOY A COLORTASTIC BREAK WITH !
+ BONUS UPSIDE DOWN EXTRAS

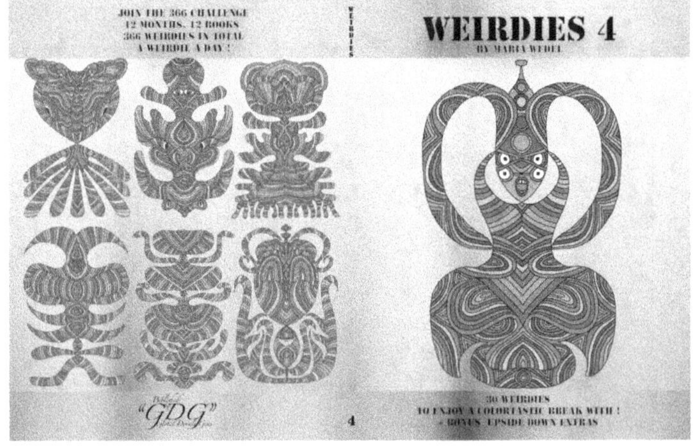
JOIN THE 366 CHALLENGE
12 MONTHS, 12 BOOKS
366 WEIRDIES IN TOTAL
A WEIRDIE A DAY !
WEIRDIES 4
BY MARIA WEDEL
"GDG"
4
30 WEIRDIES
TO ENJOY A COLORTASTIC BREAK WITH !
+ BONUS UPSIDE DOWN EXTRAS

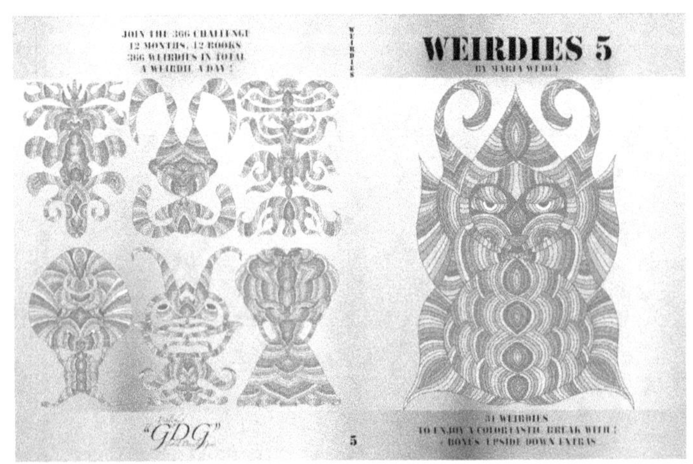
JOIN THE 366 CHALLENGE
12 MONTHS, 12 BOOKS
366 WEIRDIES IN TOTAL
A WEIRDIE A DAY !
WEIRDIES 5
BY MARIA WEDEL
"GDG"
5
31 WEIRDIES
TO ENJOY A COLORTASTIC BREAK WITH !
+ BONUS UPSIDE DOWN EXTRAS

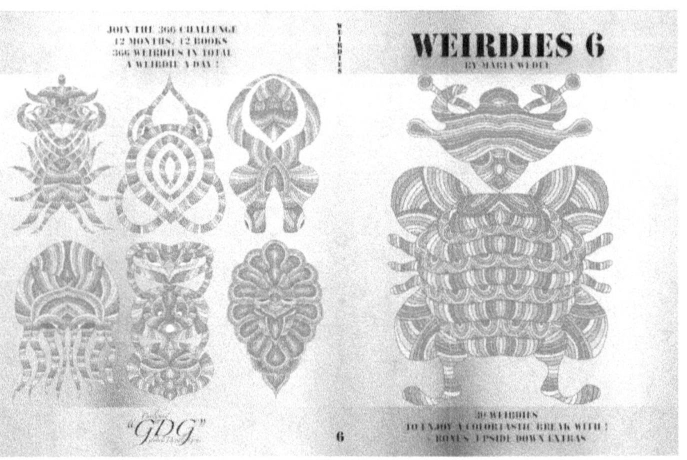
JOIN THE 366 CHALLENGE
12 MONTHS, 12 BOOKS
366 WEIRDIES IN TOTAL
A WEIRDIE A DAY !
WEIRDIES 6
BY MARIA WEDEL
"GDG"
6
30 WEIRDIES
TO ENJOY A COLORTASTIC BREAK WITH !
+ BONUS UPSIDE DOWN EXTRAS

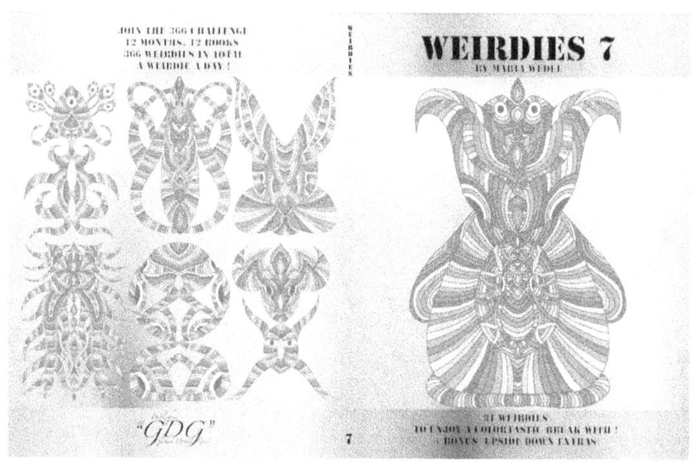

JOIN THE 366 CHALLENGE
12 MONTHS, 12 BOOKS
366 WEIRDIES IN TOTAL
A WEIRDIE A DAY!
WEIRDIES 7
BY MARIA WEDEL
"GDG"
7
31 WEIRDIES
TO ENJOY A COLORTASTIC BREAK WITH!
+ BONUS UPSIDE DOWN EXTRAS

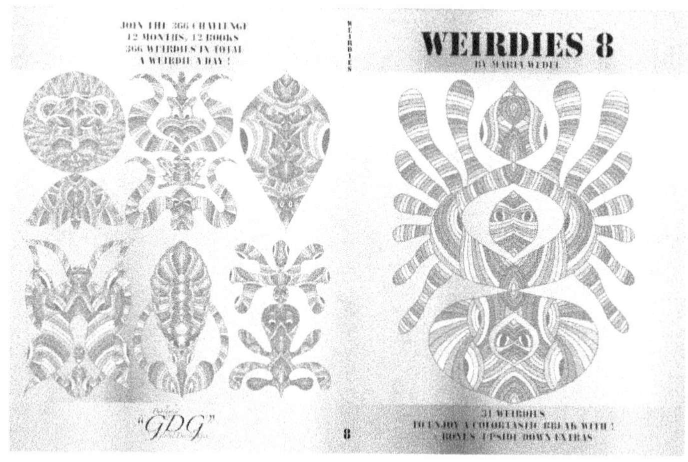

JOIN THE 366 CHALLENGE
12 MONTHS, 12 BOOKS
366 WEIRDIES IN TOTAL
A WEIRDIE A DAY!
WEIRDIES 8
BY MARIA WEDEL
"GDG"
8
31 WEIRDIES
TO ENJOY A COLORTASTIC BREAK WITH!
+ BONUS UPSIDE DOWN EXTRAS

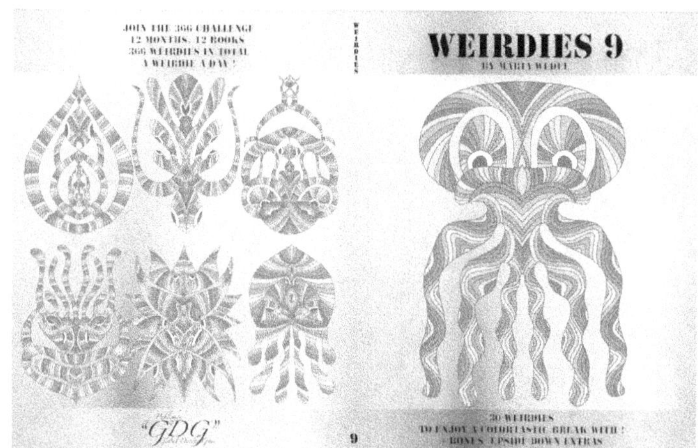

JOIN THE 366 CHALLENGE
12 MONTHS, 12 BOOKS
366 WEIRDIES IN TOTAL
A WEIRDIE A DAY!
WEIRDIES 9
BY MARIA WEDEL
"GDG"
9
30 WEIRDIES
TO ENJOY A COLORTASTIC BREAK WITH!
+ BONUS UPSIDE DOWN EXTRAS

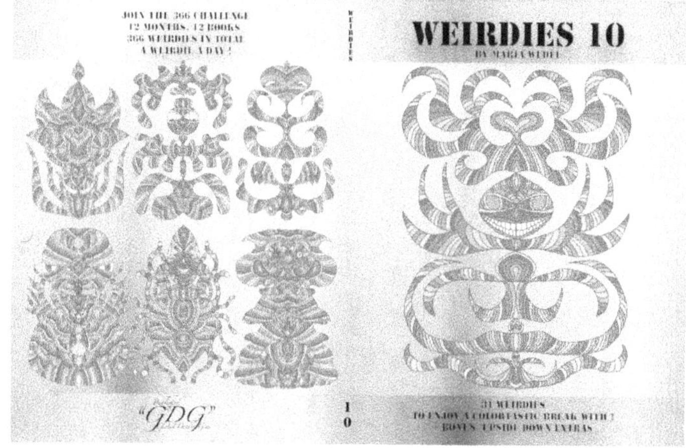

JOIN THE 366 CHALLENGE
12 MONTHS, 12 BOOKS
366 WEIRDIES IN TOTAL
A WEIRDIE A DAY!
WEIRDIES 10
BY MARIA WEDEL
"GDG"
10
31 WEIRDIES
TO ENJOY A COLORTASTIC BREAK WITH!
+ BONUS UPSIDE DOWN EXTRAS

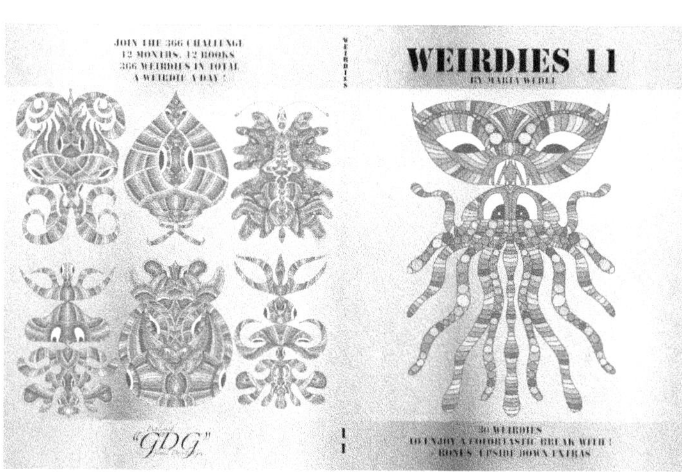

JOIN THE 366 CHALLENGE
12 MONTHS, 12 BOOKS
366 WEIRDIES IN TOTAL
A WEIRDIE A DAY!
WEIRDIES 11
BY MARIA WEDEL
"GDG"
11
30 WEIRDIES
TO ENJOY A COLORTASTIC BREAK WITH!
+ BONUS UPSIDE DOWN EXTRAS

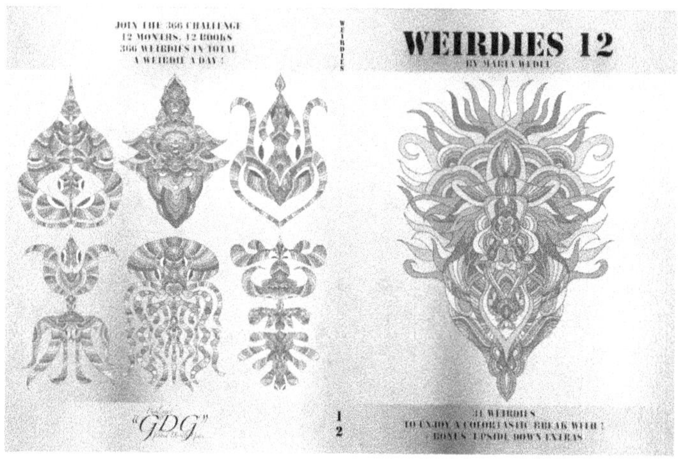

JOIN THE 366 CHALLENGE
12 MONTHS, 12 BOOKS
366 WEIRDIES IN TOTAL
A WEIRDIE A DAY!
WEIRDIES 12
BY MARIA WEDEL
"GDG"
12
31 WEIRDIES
TO ENJOY A COLORTASTIC BREAK WITH!
+ BONUS UPSIDE DOWN EXTRAS